제나쌤의
영어리스닝
길잡이

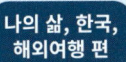
**나의 삶, 한국,
해외여행 편**

**유튜브 채널 [길잡이영어]
[봄봄클래스] 강의교재**

제나(김주언) 지음

길잡이★북스

국내파 영어전공자의 첫번째 난관 - 리스닝

'듣고, 듣고, 또, 듣고 한 100번 반복해 들으면, 쌀라쌀라 훅~ 지나가는 이 영어도 언젠간 들리는 날이 오겠지?'

'아니, 아예 백지를 펴고, 들리는 걸 죄다 받아써 보자. 계속 돌려 들으면 다 잡아낼 수 있을 거야!'

소위 국내파로서 대학에서 영어를 전공하며 가장 어려웠던 부분은 다름 아닌 리스닝이었다.

경북 영주라는 작은 지방 소도시에서 나름 대학수능 영어도 만점 받고, 고등학교 영어 스피치 대회에서 최우수상도 타고, 학창 시절, 아침 6시에 일어나 당시 인기 있던 라디오방송 〈굿모닝팝스〉도 꼬박꼬박 챙겨듣고 중얼중얼 따라 하며 '오~ 영어 재밌다! 할만한데?' 하던, 우물 안 행복한 개구리가 나였다.

영어를 좋아해 자연스럽게 대학에서 영어를 전공하게 되었고, 1학년 1학기 때, '이 정도는 들어야 영어과라 할 수 있지' 싶어 호기롭게 미국인 교수님의 역사 관련 교양수업을 듣게 되었다. 첫 수업을 듣는데, 쌀라쌀라 훅~ 쌀라쌀라 훅훅~ 으잉? 뭐지? 왜 안 들리지? 앞부분이 좀 들린다 싶으면 뒷부분이 훅~ 지나가고 어떤 부분은 아예 앞부분부터 안 들렸다.

큰. 일. 났. 다. 망. 했. 다……

리스닝과의 사투 - 무조건 반복청취!

발등에 떨어진 불을 끄기 위해, 나는 영어방송을 듣고 또 들었다. 심지어

소리내어 읽으면 영어가 들린다

제나쌤의
영어리스닝
길잡이

나의 삶, 한국,
해외여행 편

1권

유튜브 채널 [길잡이영어]
[봄봄클래스] 강의교재

제나(김주연) 지음

전)EBS강사 제나쌤이 알려주는
효과만점 영어귀뚫기 7단계 학습법

영어 학습 콘텐츠
유튜브 채널 [길잡이영어]

제나쌤 온라인 강의
[봄봄클래스]

길잡이★북스

백지를 펴고 영어 음원을 듣고, 그대로 적는 받아쓰기(dictation)도 시작했다. 일단 들리는 부분은 적고, 안 들리는 부분은 되감기를 해서 반복해 들으면서 비어있는 부분을 채워나가는 식이었다.

근데 문제는, 안 들리는 부분은 아무리 반복해 들어도 안 들린다는 거였다. 정말이지 답답했다. 안되겠다 싶어 영어학원 청취반도 등록했다. 당시 인기있던 미국드라마 〈프렌즈〉를 교재 삼아 그날 배울 내용을 들려준 뒤, 스크립트를 나눠주고 간략히 내용을 훑어준 다음, 앵무새처럼 반복해서 음원을 따라 쉐도잉(그대로 따라 읽기) 하는 방식의 수업이었다. 하지만, 이 방식은 불행히도 내게 그다지 효과가 없었다.

예상치 못한 돌파구 - 같은 국내파 친구의 조언

'빠르고 긴 영어가 들리려면 다시 태어나야 하나?' '역시, 어릴 때 해외에서 살아야 하나보다'하며 심란해 하고 있던 차에, 나에게 지나가는 말로 조언을 해 준 친구가 있었다. 나 같은 국내파 영어과 동기인데, 영어를 너무 잘하는 친구였다. 다들 그 친구가 영어로 말하면, 해외 어딘가에서 살다 온 줄 알았나. 하루는 그 친구에게 평소 영어 공부를 어떻게 하냐고 물어봤다. 그러자 그 친구 왈,

"나는 내가 보는 모든 영어 문장은 소리 내 읽어봐, 심지어 고등학교 때 수능 영어 문제집도 다 풀고 나서는 꼭 소리 내어 읽어봤어. 남들이 단어를 쓰면서 외울 때, 난 소리 내 읽어가며 외웠어. 내 입이 내는 소리를 내 귀가 듣도록"

'뭐야, 이렇게 간단하다고? 그냥 소리 내어 읽으라고? 근데 한번 해보자,

밑져야 본전이니까. 그냥 한번 해보자.'

매일 영어를 소리내어 읽었더니 생긴 놀라운 변화들

그날부터 나는 내가 공부하는 영어 지문들을 읽기 시작했다. 시간 관계상 모든 지문을 읽지는 못하겠지만, 그날 배운 내용 중 괜찮아 보이는 내용의 지문은 눈으로 한 단어 한 단어 쫓아가며, 정성스럽게 영혼을 담아서 반드시 소리 내 읽었다.

그런데, 읽으면 읽을수록, 한 가지 재미있는 걸 알게 됐다. 눈으로 쓱 보고 이해되면 지나치고, 막히면 잠깐 멈췄다 또 지나치던, 그저 그런 영어 문장들이, 입으로 소리 내어 읽기 시작하니 뭐랄까, 귀에 인이 박히는 느낌이 들었다. 키보드를 두드리면 글자들이 모니터에 하나씩 찍히듯, 영어 소리가 귀에 타닥타닥 발자국처럼 남는 기분이랄까.

무엇보다 그렇게 한번 직접 읽고 나서 음원을 들으면, 그때는 정말이지 들리는 게 달.랐.다. 내가 읽은 발음이나 억양, 리듬이 원어민 음원과 같으면 너무 뿌듯했고, 그 부분은 당연히 잘 들렸다. 근데 내가 '이렇게 소리 나겠지?' 했던 부분이 원어민 음원과 다르면 나도 모르게 귀가 쫑긋, 그 다른 부분에 더 집중하게 됐다.

내가 제대로 못 읽어낸 부분을 눈으로는 스크립트를 보면서, 어떻게 소리 나는지를 다시 재생해서 들었다. 그리고 내 소리와 원어민 음원 소리 사이의 차이를 잡아냈다. 아니 차이가 느껴졌다. '아, 이 부분은 이렇게 소리 나네, 억양이 여기가 올라가고 여기가 내려가네.' 이렇게 내가 눈으로 보고 있는 텍스트들이 실제 어떻게 소리화되는지 점점 감이 쌓여갔다. 영어 발음과 억양이 더욱 자연스러워짐은 물론이었다.

　뿐만 아니었다. 소리 내어 읽기를 하면 할수록, 영어 구문들이 익숙해지고 또 복잡한 영어 어순이 머릿속에 정리가 되어가는 기분이었다. (영어에서 가장 어려운 부분 중 하나가 바로 이 어순 아닌가!)

　사실, 어떤 글을 내 입으로 직접 소리 내어 읽으려면, 눈앞의 문장들을 한 자 한 자 더욱 집중해서 봐야 한다. 주어 + 동사로 시작되는 평서문은 물론이고, 휙 지나가 잘 안들리는 의문사로 시작되는 각종 의문문 등, 그냥 눈으로만 봤으면 슥~ 훑고 지나갔을 영어 문장들이 눈에도 콱콱, 머릿속에 발자국이 찍히는 기분이 들었다. 어순이 눈으로도 익숙해지고, 입으로도 익숙해지니, 그 뒤부터는 귀로 들어도 바로바로 내용이 이해가 갔다. 이 또한 아주 신비로운 경험이었다.

　이후 나는 그냥 음원을 틀어놓고 마냥 듣는 게 아니라, 소리 내어 읽고 듣기를 '한 세트'로 공부했다. 그리자 정말이지 하루가 다르게 점점, 예선에 틀어두고 흘려듣던 영어방송들이 조금씩 들리기 시작했다. (여기서 '들린다'는 말은 소리가 인식되며, 동시에 내용도 이해가 된다는 말이다.)
　정말이지 놀라운 체험이었다. '소리 내어 읽으니 들리는 구나!'

소리 내어 읽기 - 누구나 가능하다!
　근데, 이 방법이 내 친구와 나만 되는 거라면? 누구나 이 방법으로 리스닝이 된다는 검증이 필요했다. 나는 이후 개인수업으로 가르치던 학생들에게 그날의 영어교재 지문을 소리 내어 읽고 녹음하는 걸 매일 숙제로 내주고 확인했다.

대부분의 학생들은 자기 목소리를 녹음하여 듣는 것이 너무 낯설고 어색해서 처음에는 이 방법을 다소 껄끄러워했다. 하지만 대략 6개월 정도 지나면, 학생들의 듣기 실력은 말할 것도 없고, 리딩 실력까지 눈에 띄게 좋아졌다.

무엇보다 학생들 스스로가 영어가 어떤 느낌의 언어인지 조금씩 감이 오기 시작한다고 했다. 사실, 이게 가장 중요하지 않은가? 영어에 대한 감을 잡는 거! 학생들이 나와 같은 수순을 밟아가는 게 보였다. 그냥 입을 꾹 닫고 눈으로만 읽는 것이 아닌, 내 입으로 직접 소리 내 읽어서, 내가 낸 소리를 내 귀가 듣게 하는 방법. 이 방법으로 누구나 영어가 늘 수 있다는 확신이 생겼다. 영어 귀가 트이려면, 아니 영어라는 어려운 외국어에 익숙해지려면 소리 내어 읽는 게 아주 중요하다는 큰 깨달음이었다.

리딩-리스닝-스피킹 All-in-One 통합수업으로의 확장

사실, 지난 15년 넘게 현장에서 영어강사로서, 다양한 연령대의 학습자들을 가르치면서 알게 된 점은, 많은 학습자들이 영어자료들을 입을 꾹 닫고 눈으로만 이해해거나, 아니면 각종 음원들을 역시 입을 꾹 닫고 귀로만 반복해 듣는다는 것이었다.

어떤 언어를 구사한다는 것은 눈으로 보고, 귀로 듣고, 입으로 말하는, 이 모든 것이 동시에 하나로 연결된 것이건만, 실상은 리딩 따로, 리스닝 따로, 스피킹 따로, 모두 분절된 채 너무도 비효율적으로 공부를 하고 있는 사람들이 예전의 나를 비롯해 너무나 많다는 것을 현장수업에서 알게 되었다.

이후 나는 내 수업 방식의 틀을 보다 체계적으로 잡아나갔다. 우선, 그날 교재 본문에 나온 문장들을 하나하나 파악이 되게끔, 그리고 거기 나온 주요 문장구조나 회화에 자주 쓰이는 패턴이 익숙해지고, 나아가 응용이 가능할 정도로 충분히 연습시켰다. 나는 이걸 가리켜 '문장공부'라는 나만의 이름을 붙였다.

그 다음, 충분히 이해가 된 그날의 본문을 의미 단위로 끊어 읽기를 통해 어떻게 읽어나가는지 단어의 발음이며, 여러 단어들의 연음, 문장의 억양과 리듬 등을 가르쳤다. 나는 이걸 '소리공부'라 부른다. 그런 다음, 혼자서 쭉 말하는 서술문의 경우는 혼자서, 둘이서 짝을 지어 이야기하는 대화문의 경우 둘이서, 이렇게 해당 본문은 반드시 학생들이 직접 소리 내어 읽게끔 했다.

마지막으로 그날 본문 주제나 상황을 응용해서, 이와 관련해 학생들에게 적용할 만한 질문을 하나 만들고, 이에 대해 나올법한 대답 몇 가지를 영어로 어떻게 말하는지 먼저 일러준 뒤, 그 뒤 파트너와 시로 묻고 답히며 스피킹까지 연습하는, 일명 All-in-One 통합수업을 했다.

이런 방식의 수업은 무엇보다 현장에서 학생들 반응이 아주 좋았다. 무엇보다 영어가 재미있다고, 눈으로 이해되는 문장이 늘어가고, 들리는 문장이 늘어가고, 무엇보다 조금씩 관련 주제로 말까지 할 수 있게 되니까 영어가 재미있어졌다는 분들이 점점 많아졌다.

특히, 내가 주로 가르친 학생들은, 원어민 선생님 반에 가기 전인, 초급에서 중급까지의 학습자들이 대부분이었는데, 20대 대학생부터 70대 어르신들까지 연령을 불문하고, 영어를 배워가고 영어가 늘어가는데 재미를 느낀다는 반응에 정말이지 강사로서 기쁘고 보람된 시간들이었다.

유튜브 길잡이영어, 그리고 봄봄클래스의 시작

그러던 중 코로나19가 발생했고, 개인적으로는 출산과 육아로 인해 현장 강의를 잠시 쉬게 되었다. 이때 마침 유튜브 제작이라는 새로운 기회를 만나게 되었다.

'영어를 제대로 다시 배워보고 싶은데, 어디서부터 어떻게 해야 할지 몰라 막막하다'는 분들에게 도움이 되는 영상을 만들어보고자 하는 취지에서 [길잡이영어] 채널을 시작하게 되었다.

더불어, 지난 15년간의 강의 경험을 바탕으로, 제대로 된 영어강의를 만들어보자는 생각에 제작하게 된 강의가 바로, 이 교재를 바탕으로 한 〈봄봄클래스〉다.

〈봄봄클래스〉는 나에게 일어날 법한 상황과, 외국인과 대화할 때 나올 만한 주제에 대해 바로 써먹을 수 있도록 준비시켜주는 60강으로 이루어진 강의다.

- 한국에서 가장 많은 레벨인 초중급(초급에서 중급 사이) 학습자 대상
- 리딩–리스닝–스피킹을 한 번에 배울 수 있는 All-in-One 통합수업
- 초중급 학습자들이 꼭 배워야 할 실용적인 생활밀착형 주제와 내용
  - 일상생활
  - 나의 살아온 삶과 경험
  - 앞으로의 계획 말하기

- 한국에 대한 이야기
- 해외여행 상황별 회화

이 책의 강의 목차를 꼭 한번 봐주시길 바란다. 이 주제들을 모두 다룬 영어교재는 없다고 감히 자부한다. 지난 15년간 가르쳐 온 수많은 영어교재들을 바탕으로, 한국인 학습자가 미리 공부해놓으면 도움 될만한 주제와 내용들로 꽉꽉 채워 담아놓았다. 이 책은 내 15년 강의자료 모음집이나 다름없다.

이 책을 펴는 당신께

    <봄봄클래스> 강의에서 PDF 문서로 제공되었던 강의자료들을 책으로 출간하면 좋겠다는 학습자분들의 요청으로, 이제 이 수업자료들이 교재로 세상에 나오게 되었다. 혹시, 소리 내어 읽기를 통해 영어를 공부하고 싶은데, '어디서 뭐부터 읽으면 좋을까?' 하는 분들이 있다면, 이 책을 권해 드린다.

    또한 '이 책을 가지고 이떻게 공부해야 하나?' 묻는 분을 위해, 다음 페이지부터 <이 책의 활용법>을 아주 자세히 준비했다. 꼭 시간을 내어 한 번 읽어보신 뒤, 이 책을 200% 활용하시길 바란다.

    마지막으로, 이 책과 <봄봄클래스> 강의가 오랜 시간 영어를 공부해도 제자리인 분들, 영어를 잘하고 싶은데 어디서부터 뭘 어떻게 해야 할지 막막한 분들에게, 조금이나마 도움이 되길 바라며, 여러분의 영어여정을 온 마음으로 응원한다.

- 제나 (김주연)

이 책의 활용법

- 이 책은 유튜브 [길잡이영어] 채널 제나쌤의 <봄봄클래스> 강의 교재로서, 강의와 함께 공부했을 때, 그 효과를 극대화할 수 있습니다.
- 각 페이지 상단 오른쪽의 QR코드로 해당 음원을 들을 수 있습니다. 스마트폰 카메라나 QR코드 인식 앱으로 촬영하면 음원에 바로 연결됩니다.
- 이 책을 독학으로 공부하실 경우, 아래의 단계와 방법대로 공부해 보시길 권장합니다.

<제나쌤의 효과 만점 영어 귀뚫기 7단계>

1단계 음원은 딱 1번만 듣고, 바로 스크립트(본문) 펴기

2단계 **눈으로** 문장 꼼꼼히 파악 및 내용 이해하기

3단계 본문 처음부터 끝까지, 일단 아는 선에서 **입으로** 소리 내어 읽어보기

4단계 스크립트 펴고 **눈으로** 보면서 동시에 **귀로** 들어보기

5단계 의미 단위로 끊어서 **입으로** 소리 내어 읽기 연습하기

6단계 본문 처음부터 끝까지 쭉 한 번에 다시 **입으로** 소리 내어 읽어보기

7단계 스크립트 덮고 **귀로만** 음원 들어보기

<독학을 위한 보다 자세한 귀뚫기 7단계 학습법>

본문 학습하기

1단계 음원은 딱 1번만 듣고, 바로 스크립트(본문) 펴기

한 번 듣고 안 들리는 건, 여러 번 반복해 들어도 안 들릴 확률이 높다. 스크립트를 눈으로 봤는데 무슨 내용인지 이해가 안 가든, 소리 자체를 인식하지 못해서든, 이유가 뭐가 됐든 마찬가지다. 처음에 듣고 이해가 안 가면 바로 과감히 스크립트를 편다!

2단계 눈으로 문장 꼼꼼히 파악 및 내용 이해하기 (문장공부)

대충 슥~ 눈으로 훑고 무슨 내용인지 대략 알겠다 하는 걸로는 부족하다. 눈으로 대충 파악한 문장은, 귀로 들어도 대충 스쳐가며 들린다. 또한 이렇게 대충 봐 버릇한 문장은, 나중에 절대 입 밖으로 안 나온다. 스피킹 공부는 나중에 또 따로 해야 한다는 뜻이기도 하다. 한 문장 한 문장 꼼꼼히 파악해서, 이 문장을 내가 나중에 어딘가에서 직접 말할 수 있겠다는 정도로 공부해놔야 한다. (별표 다섯 개! ★★★★★)

더불어, 문장을 볼 때, 앞에서부터 쭉쭉 읽어가며 바로바로 이해하는 "직독직해" 스킬을 늘려야 한다. 우리가 한국어로 된 글을 읽을 때 그냥 쭉쭉 앞에서부터 읽으며 바로바로 이해하지 않나? 마찬가지다. 원어민이 영어로 된 글을 읽을 때 어떻게 읽어나갈지 상상하면서, 바로바로 연필 가는 속도 대로 쭉쭉 이해해 나가는 리딩 스킬을 키워야 한다.

혼자 리딩이 가능한 사람은 독학으로 매 강에 나온 본문을 공부하면 되고,

이 독해 부분이 어려운 중급 이하의 학습자들에게는 〈봄봄클래스〉강의 중 본문 설명(리딩) 부분을 꼼꼼히 공부해서 리딩 스킬을 늘릴 것을 권장한다.

그런데 여기서, 영어 문장을 꼼꼼히 공부한다는 건 무슨 뜻일까?
1) 영어는 동사가 아주 중요하고, 이 동사가 어떻게 활용되는지 잘 익혀둬야 한다.

(예문)

① **I want to exercise regularly.** (나는 규칙적으로 운동하고 싶다.)
⇒ want to 동사: (동사)하기를 원하다

한국인들이 무난하게 보고, 듣고, 이해하는 문장이다.

② **I want you to exercise regularly.** (나는 네가 규칙적으로 운동했으면 한다.)
⇒ want A to 동사: A가 (동사)하기를 원하다

이 I want you to (동사) 구문은, 바라는 건 '나'지만, 그 행동을 하는 건 '너'인 경우다. (= 난 말이지, 네가 ~했으면 좋겠다) 회화에서 많이 나오는데, 한국인 학습자 입장에서는 눈에 익숙해지고 입에 익숙해지는데 연습이 필요한 구문이다. 딱 들었을 때, 바로 이해가 되려면, 먼저 눈으로 충분히 익숙해져야 한다.

③ **Do you want me to give you a ride?** (너 내가 태워다 주기를 바래?)
⇒ 위의 ②번과 같은 구문인데, 의문문이라 어렵게 느껴진다.

Do you want me to (동사)? 쉽게 말해, "내가 (동사) 해줄까?"의 뜻이다. 먼저 눈으로 충분히 익숙해질 때까지 들여다보고, 입으로도 반복해서 말해봐야 한다.

④ **What do you want me to do?** (너 내가 뭘 해주기를 바래?)
　⇒ (직역) 무엇을 / 너는 / 내가 해주길 원해?

　미드나 영화 대사에 종종 나오는 문장인데, 모국어로 자연스럽게 배우지 않으면 한 번에 딱 느낌이 안 오는 문장이다. (내가 그랬다!) 이런 문장은 딱 보면 바로 한 눈에 이해가 갈 정도로 익혀놔야, 귀로 들어도 바로 이해가 딱 된다.

2) 영어에서 어떤 단어를 처음 봤을 때는, 단지 그 뜻만이 아니라, 그 단어가 어떤 단어와 함께 연결되어 짝꿍처럼 쓰이는지 단어의 쓰임을 잘 봐둬야 한다. (이 표현을 이용해 나중에 말로 하라면 할 수 있을 정도가 목표다.)

　예를 들어, 'be interested'는 '관심이 있다, 흥미가 있다' 뜻이지만, '~에 관심이 있다, 흥미가 있다' 할 때는 뒤에 연결어로 전치사 in이 항상 짝꿍처럼 붙어서 나온다. 'be interested in' '~에 관심이 있다, 흥미가 있다'
　또한, 이 in과 같은 전치사 뒤에는,
① 명사나
② 대명사의 목적격, 나아가 동사가 올 경우는,
③ 동사ing (동명사)가 온다는 것까지 알아두면 좋다.

(예문)

① **I'm interested in history.** (명사)
　나는 역사에 관심이 있어.
② **I'm interested in him.** (대명사가 올 경우 목적격)
　나는 그 남자에게 관심이 있어.
③ **I'm interested in cooking.** (동사ing - 동명사)
　나는 요리하는 것에 관심이 있어.

발음을 전혀 모르는 생소한 단어가 있다 해도 일단 추정해서 읽어보자. '이렇게 소리 나려나?' 대충 유추해서 읽어본다. 이 단계는 생각보다 아주 중요한데, 이렇게 한번 내 힘으로 직접 소리 내어 읽어보면, 생각보다 더듬더듬 버벅대는 부분이 많다고 느껴질 것이다. (당신이 중급 이하의 학습자라면 더더욱 그럴 것이다.) 그럴 때는 좌절하지 말고, 역으로 이렇게 생각하라. '아~ 이래서 안 들렸구나, 눈으로 보고도 제대로 못 읽어내는 글을 원어민이 빠르게 쌀라쌀라 말했으니, 들릴 리가 없지. 당연한 거구나, 놀랄 게 없네.' 이렇게 말이다.

참고로, 수학 문제 풀 때도 일단 내 힘으로 풀어보고, 그 뒤에 선생님의 풀이나 해설지를 봐야 내가 막혔던 부분에 대해 깨달음과 발전이 있는 법이다. 영어도 마찬가지! 일단 내가 아는 모든 영어 발음에 대한 지식을 총동원해, 일단 한번 본문을 더듬더듬이라도 끝까지 읽어본다.

여기서 중요한 건 '스크립트를 펴고'다. 눈으로 아까 배운 본문 텍스트를 보면서 동시에 귀로 들어보며 '아~ 이 단어가 이렇게 소리 나는구나', '으잉? 이 부분은 내가 생각했던 소리가 아니네? 너무 다른데?' 이런 식으로 내가 미처 몰랐던 부분, 내 소리와 음원 소리의 '차이'를 느껴보는 게 이 단계의 핵심이다. 이 '차이'가 느껴져야 거기서부터 발전이 시작된다.

이걸 전문용어로 '메타인지'라고 하는데, 쉽게 말해, 내가 무엇을 알고 무엇을 모르는지를 객관적으로 파악하는 능력을 말한다. 이 메타인지가 발달

할수록, 영어학습에 있어서 보다 주도적으로, 또한 효과적으로 나의 부족한 부분을 파악하고 개선해 나갈 수 있다.

5단계 의미 단위로 끊어서 입으로 소리 내어 읽기 연습하기 (소리공부)

영어는 단순히 줄줄 읽거나 말하는 언어가 아니다. 의미 단위로 끊어 읽고, 그 안에서 강세(힘주어 또렷하게 발음하는 부분)를 중심으로, 소리가 올라가고 내려가며, 빠르게 혹은 길게 읽는, 억양과 리듬이 형성된다. 이러한 영어 특유의 소리에 익숙해져야 비로소 영어가 들리기 시작한다. (여기도 별표 다섯 개! ★★★★★)

이 책의 "소리 내어 읽기" 코너에는 의미 단위로 끊어읽는 표시(/)가 되어 있다. 이를 참고해서 읽어보되, 독학하는 경우는 소리를 유추해서 읽어보고, 모르는 단어 발음은 네이버 사전 같은 사전앱이나 ChatGPT 같은 AI앱을 통해 알아본다. 또한, 아직 영어 억양과 리듬을 살려가며 끊어 읽는다는 게 어떤 건지 잘 모르겠는 경우, 이 책을 교재로 강의하는 〈봄봄클래스〉 강의의 끊어 읽기 연습 부분을 집중적으로 공부하길 권한다.

(참고) 혹자는 음원을 그대로 따라 하는 '쉐도잉'이 리스닝 실력 향상에 더 좋지 않냐고 하는데, 쉐도잉도 물론 도움이 된다. 하지만, 둘 다 해본 내 경험상, 쉐도잉보다 효과가 좋은 게 바로 이 소리 내어 읽기다. 쉐도잉은 자칫하면, 그냥 아무 생각 없이 음원 소리를 카피하는 '앵무새'가 되기 쉽다. 소리를 그대로 흉내 낼 수 있다고 그 언어를 잘하는 게 아니다. 어떤 앵무새가 "안녕하세요"라는 말을 너무나 자연스럽게 잘 내뱉는다고 해서, 그 앵무새더러 한국어 정말 잘한다 하지 않는 것처럼 말이다.

또한, 쉐도잉보다 소리 내어 읽기가 리스닝에 더 효과적인 이유는, 내가 지금 눈으로 봐서 이해가 되는 이 텍스트가 어떻게 소리화되는지, 내가 미리 '능동적으로' 생각하며 읽어봐야, 나중에 음원을 들었을 때, 잘못 알고 있거나 못 읽는 발음 혹은 연음을 바로 알아챌 수 있기 때문이다.

나의 경우도 이 소리 내어 읽기를 하고부터 '귀가 트여간다'라는 체험을 비로소 하기 시작했다. 그날 열심히 들고파며 배운 영어 본문은 무조건 소리 내어 읽어라!

6단계 본문 처음부터 끝까지 쭉 한 번에 다시 입으로 소리 내어 읽어보기

의미 단위로 끊어 끊어 연습하던 본문을, 이제 다시 모두 붙여서 처음부터 끝까지 쭉 다시 한번 읽어본다. 맨 처음 무턱대고 읽었던 아까보다는 좀 더 술술 읽게 되는 것을 느낄 수 있을 것이다. (행여 잘 안된다 하더라도 좌절금지다. 오늘 처음 본 문장들 아닌가! 유창하게 술술 읽힌다면 당신은 언어천재다. 복습삼아 여러 번 반복해 읽으면, 점점 나아진다. 이 또한 나의 체험담이다.)

7단계 스크립트(본문) 덮고 귀로만 음원 들어보기

이제야말로 스크립트를 덮고, 오직 귀로만 들어본다. 한 구간, 한 구간 나오는 소리를 인지해 보고, 그 소리가 어떤 내용인지도 느껴본다. 아직 잘 안 들린다면, 다시 1단계-6단계를 해보거나, 내용(본문 문장들)이 충분히 인지가 되었다면, 3단계-6단계를 반복한다. 중요한 것은, 그냥 반복해 듣는 게 아니라, 내 입으로 직접 소리내어 읽은 뒤 들어보는 걸 "한 세트"로 한다는 것이다. 이러면 정말 영어 귀가 점점 트인다. 내 강사경력을 걸고 보증

한다.

15년 넘는 경력의 영어강사로서, 무엇보다 나 자신이 한국에서 나고 자라, 모국어가 아닌, 외국어로 영어를 배운 사람으로, 나는 "눈"으로 시작해서 (리딩), "입"으로 이어지고(낭독), "귀"로 마무리되는(리스닝), 이 7단계 학습법이 성인학습자가 영어를 배우는 최고의 학습법이라 자부한다.

스피킹1_ 중요 패턴 익히기 학습하기

각 강에 나오는 중요 패턴을 하나 뽑고, 실생활 활용도가 높은 예문들을 수록했다. 특히, 강을 더해갈수록 단순한 패턴 한 문장이 아니라, 그 문장 전후로 어떤 문장이 올 수 있을지, 맥락에 맞게 추가해 보았다. 우선, 중요 패턴을 익힌 뒤, 영어 예문과 뒤에 나오는 한국어 해석 문장을 대조해 보면서, 어떤 느낌으로 그 패턴이 쓰이는지 감을 잡아보자. 그 후 소리 내어 읽어보고, 마지막으로 큐알코드의 해당 음원을 들어보자.

스피킹2_ [내 이야기해 봅시다] 학습하기

각 강의 상황이나 주제를 응용하여, '내 이야기'를 할 수 있게끔 응용 실문과, 나올 법한 대답 몇 가지를 꾸며 보았다. 이 부분은 현장수업하면서, 특히 한국인 학습자들이 공통적으로 많이 하던 대답을 떠올리며 만들어보았다. '외국인과 대화할 때 이런 질문을 해 볼 수 있고, 또 이런 대답을 할 수 있겠다' 상상하며 연습해 보면 좋다. 이 역시 영어 예문과 뒤에 나오는 한국어 해석 부분을 함께 보면서, '이 말은 영어로 이렇게 하면 되네'라는 느낌으로 감을 잡아본 뒤, 소리 내어 읽어보고 마지막으로 큐알코드 해당 음원을 들어본다.

CONTENTS

👁 **본문 눈으로 이해하기**

Alice : Hi! Are you Jinsu?

Jinsu : Yes, that's me! You must be Alice. We connected on the language exchange app, right?

Alice : That's right! Great to meet you. It's nice to finally meet you in person.

Jinsu : Nice to meet you, too. I've been looking forward to meeting you.

(Kevin walks up to Alice)

Alice : Oh, Jinsu, this is my brother, Kevin. Kevin, this is Jinsu.

Kevin : Hi, Jinsu! Nice to meet you.

Jinsu : Nice to meet you too, Kevin. Are you visiting Alice?

Kevin : Yes, I am! I'm visiting from Chicago. I'm just here to see Alice and explore a bit.

Jinsu : That's awesome! I hope you're enjoying your time here.

Kevin : I am, thank you! Alice told me that you're helping each other with language practice.

Jinsu : Yes, exactly! She's so good at explaining things.

👄 본문 소리 내어 읽기

Alice : Hi! Are you Jinsu?

Jinsu : Yes, that's me! You must be Alice. We connected **/** on the language exchange app, **/** right?

Alice : That's right! Great to meet you. It's nice to finally meet you **/** in person.

Jinsu : Nice to meet you, too. I've been looking forward to meeting you.

(Kevin walks up to Alice)

Alice : Oh, Jinsu, this is my brother, Kevin. Kevin, this is Jinsu.

Kevin : Hi, Jinsu! Nice to meet you.

Jinsu : Nice to meet you too, Kevin. Are you visiting Alice?

Kevin : Yes, I am! I'm visiting from Chicago. I'm just here **/** to see Alice and explore a bit.

Jinsu : That's awesome! I hope **/** you're enjoying your time here.

Kevin : I am, thank you! Alice told me **/** that you're helping each other **/** with language practice.

Jinsu : Yes, exactly! She's so good at explaining things.

1강 소개하기

⬤ 스피킹1_ 중요 패턴 익히기

help A with B(명사/동사ing) : A를 B에 대해 돕다

- Can you help me with my homework? It's due tomorrow but I'm stuck now.

- If you're okay with it, I'll help you with the project.

- She helped me with that issue and it worked out well.

🗣 **스피킹2_ 내 이야기해 봅시다**

Q Is there anything you're looking forward to right now?

A
- Yes, I'm looking forward to my family trip to Guam.

- Of course. I'm looking forward to moving to my new apartment.

- Not really. Nothing comes to mind at the moment.

1강　소개하기

◎ 본문 [해석]

Alice : 안녕하세요! 혹시 진수 씨인가요?

Jinsu : 네, 맞아요! 당신이 앨리스죠? 우리 언어교환 앱에서 연결됐었죠, 맞죠?

Alice : 맞아요! 만나서 반가워요. 이렇게 직접 만나게 되어 정말 좋네요.

Jinsu : 저도 만나서 반갑습니다. 정말 만나고 싶었어요.

　　　　(케빈이 앨리스에게 다가온다.)

Alice : 아, 진수 씨, 이 사람은 제 남동생 케빈이에요. 케빈, 여긴 진수 씨야.

Kevin : 안녕하세요, 진수 씨! 만나서 반가워요.

Jinsu : 저도 만나서 반갑습니다. 케빈 씨. 앨리스를 보러 오신 건가요?

Kevin : 네, 맞아요! 저는 시카고에서 왔어요. 앨리스를 만나고, 조금 둘러보려고 왔습니다.

Jinsu : 멋지네요! 여기에서 즐거운 시간 보내고 계시길 바라요.

Kevin : 네, 잘 지내고 있어요. 고마워요! 앨리스가 당신이랑 언어 연습을 하고 있다고 말해 줬어요.

Jinsu : 네, 맞아요! 앨리스는 설명을 정말 잘해요.

🫦 스피킹1_ 중요 패턴 익히기 [해석]

help A with B(명사/동사ing) : A를 B에 대해 돕다

- 내 숙제 좀 도와줄 수 있어? 내일까지 제출해야 하는데 지금 막혔어.

- 네가 괜찮다면 내가 그 프로젝트를 도와줄게.

- 그녀가 그 문제를 도와줬고 잘 해결됐어.

🫦 스피킹2_ 내 이야기해 봅시다 [해석]

질문 지금 기대하고 있는 일이 있나요?

답
- 네, 가족과 함께 괌으로 여행 가는 걸 기대하고 있어요.

- 물론이죠. 새 아파트로 이사하는 걸 기대하고 있어요.

- 별로요. 지금 딱히 떠오르는 건 없어요.

◉ **본문 눈으로 이해하기**

I have been waking up at 5 a.m. every day for the past three years. At first, it was really difficult, but now I'm used to it, and I enjoy it. One of the best things about waking up early is the quiet time. There are no phone calls or messages to distract me, so I can focus without interruptions. I use this time to plan my day and start it early. I also study English in the morning, which helps me improve little by little. Sometimes, I go for a short walk to refresh my mind. Waking up early has truly become a great way to start my day with energy and focus.

👄 본문 소리 내어 읽기

I have been waking up / at 5 a.m. every day / for the past three years. At first, / it was really difficult, / but now I'm used to it, / and I enjoy it. One of the best things / about waking up early / is the quiet time. There are no phone calls or messages / to distract me, / so I can focus / without interruptions. I use this time / to plan my day / and start it early. I also study English / in the morning, / which helps me improve / little by little.

Sometimes, / I go for a short walk / to refresh my mind. Waking up early / has truly become a great way / to start my day / with energy and focus.

2강 아침 일찍 일어나기

help A B(동사원형) : A가 B하도록 돕다

- She helped me solve the problem and I really appreciated it.

- Can you help me carry this? I need to move it to the kitchen.

- Let me help you clean this up. It won't take long.

스피킹2_ 내 이야기해 봅시다

Q Are you a morning person or a night person?

A ■ I'm definitely a morning person. I feel more productive in the morning.

■ I'm more of a night person. I enjoy staying up late.

■ I think I'm in between. I just go with the flow.

2강 아침 일찍 일어나기

👁 본문 [해석]

나는 지난 3년 동안 매일 아침 5시에 일어나고 있어요. 처음에는 정말 힘들었지만, 이제는 적응이 돼서 즐기고 있습니다. 아침 일찍 일어나는 것의 가장 좋은 점 중 하나는 조용한 시간이에요. 전화나 문자 같은 방해가 없어서 집중하기에 딱 좋습니다. 이 시간을 활용해 하루를 계획하고 일찍 시작할 수 있어요. 또, 영어 공부를 하면서 조금씩 실력을 키우기도 하고, 때로는 짧게 산책을 하며 머리를 맑게 합니다. 아침 일찍 일어나는 것은 에너지와 집중력을 가지고 하루를 시작하는 훌륭한 방법이 되었어요.

아침 일찍 일어나기

👄 **스피킹1_ 중요 패턴 익히기 [해석]**

help A B(동사원형) : A가 B하도록 돕다

- 그녀는 내가 문제를 해결하도록 도와줬고 정말 고마웠어.

- 이거 옮기는 거 도와줄 수 있어? 이걸 부엌으로 옮겨야 해.

- 내가 이거 치우는 거 도와줄게. 오래 걸리지 않을 거야.

👄 **스피킹2_ 내 이야기해 봅시다 [해석]**

질문 당신은 아침형 인간인가요, 아니면 저녁형 인간인가요?

답
- 저는 확실히 아침형 인간이에요. 아침에 더 생산적인 느낌이 들어요.

- 저는 더 저녁형 인간에 가까워요. 늦게까지 깨어 있는 걸 즐겨요.

- 저는 중간인 것 같아요. 그냥 흐름에 맡겨요.

3강 취미와 여가생활

Jinsu : Hey, Alice! What do you usually do in your free time?

Alice : I like running by the Han River. It's refreshing. How about you?

Jinsu : That sounds nice! I usually watch movies. I love getting lost in a good story. Do you run every day?

Alice : I try to! Running helps me clear my mind. Do you have a favorite movie genre?

Jinsu : I really enjoy action movies, but I watch all kinds. Do you usually run alone, or with others?

Alice : Sometimes alone, but I also run with my running crew. It's motivating to run together!

Jinsu : That sounds great! Let me know if you ever have a running event.

Alice : Sure, you're welcome anytime. I'll definitely keep you in mind and let you know.

👄 본문 소리 내어 읽기

Jinsu : Hey, Alice! What do you usually do / in your free time?

Alice : I like running / by the Han River. It's refreshing. How about you?

Jinsu : That sounds nice! I usually watch movies. I love getting lost / in a good story. Do you run every day?

Alice : I try to! Running helps me / clear my mind. Do you have a favorite movie genre?

Jinsu : I really enjoy action movies, / but I watch all kinds. Do you usually run alone, / or with others?

Alice : Sometimes alone, / but I also run / with my running crew. It's motivating / to run together!

Jinsu : That sounds great! Let me know / if you ever have a running event.

Alice : Sure, you're welcome anytime. I'll definitely keep you in mind / and let you know.

3강 취미와 여가생활

👄 스피킹1_ 중요 패턴 익히기

Let me know if 주어 + 동사 : ~ 한다면 알려줘

- Let me know if you need any help. I'll be happy to help.

- Thank you for listening and let me know if you have any questions.

- Take your time to think about it. Let me know if you change your mind.

👄 **스피킹2_ 내 이야기해 봅시다**

Q **What do you usually do in your free time?**

A ▪ I like watching movies and TV shows on Netflix with my family.

▪ I love hiking and enjoying the scenery.

▪ II like going around to different places and taking photos.

▪ I ike to relax at home and just chill. I work a lot during the week.

▪ I enjoy reading books with a cup of coffee.

3강 취미와 여가생활

◎ 본문 [해석]

Jinsu : 안녕, 앨리스! 여가 시간에 주로 뭐 해?

Alice : 나는 한강에서 달리는 걸 좋아해. 상쾌하거든. 넌 어때?

Jinsu : 멋지다! 나는 주로 영화 봐. 좋은 이야기에 푹 빠지는 게 좋아. 매일 뛰어?

Alice : 노력하는 편이야! 달리기는 마음을 맑게 해줘. 좋아하는 영화 장르가 있어?

Jinsu : 액션 영화를 정말 좋아해. 하지만 다양한 장르를 다 봐. 너는 주로 혼자 뛰어, 아니면 같이 뛰어?

Alice : 가끔은 혼자 뛰지만, 러닝 크루랑도 함께 뛰어. 같이 뛰면 더 동기부여가 되거든!

Jinsu : 정말 좋다! 달리기 이벤트가 있으면 알려줘.

Alice : 물론이지, 언제든 환영이야. 꼭 기억해 두었다가 알려줄게.

3강 취미와 여가생활

👄 **스피킹1_ 중요 패턴 익히기 [해석]**

Let me know if 주어 + 동사 : ~ 한다면 알려줘

- 도움이 필요하면 알려주세요. 기꺼이 도와드릴게요.

- 들어주셔서 감사합니다. 질문이 있으면 알려주세요.

- 천천히 생각해 보세요. 마음이 바뀌면 알려주세요.

👄 **스피킹2_ 내 이야기해 봅시다 [해석]**

질문 당신은 보통 자유 시간에 무엇을 하나요?

답
- 저는 가족과 함께 넷플릭스로 영화와 TV 쇼를 보는 것을 좋아해요.

- 저는 하이킹을 하며 경치를 즐기는 것을 좋아해요.

- 저는 다양한 곳을 돌아다니며 사진 찍는 것을 좋아해요.

- 저는 집에서 쉬고 그냥 편하게 있는 것을 좋아해요. 평일에는 일을 많이 하거든요.

- 저는 커피 한 잔과 함께 책을 읽는 것을 즐겨요.

 **4강**

절약하는 습관

\<How I Save Money\>

Building a habit of saving money is one of the best things I can do for my future.

It's not just about having more money. It's also about feeling safe and secure. I try to make small changes, like bringing my own coffee or cooking meals at home, which helps me save a little each day. Making a monthly budget is also helpful because it shows me exactly where my money goes, so I can make smarter choices.

This way, I'm prepared for unexpected expenses, like car repairs or medical bills, without feeling stressed. I believe that these small steps I take now will make a big difference in the future.

👄 **본문** 소리 내어 읽기

<How I Save Money>

Building a habit of saving money / is one of the best things / I can do / for my future.

It's not just about having more money. It's also about feeling safe and secure. I try to make small changes, / like bringing my own coffee / or cooking meals at home, / which helps me save / a little each day. Making a monthly budget / is also helpful / because it shows me exactly / where my money goes, / so I can make smarter choices.

This way, / I'm prepared / for unexpected expenses, / like car repairs / or medical bills, / without feeling stressed. I believe / that these small steps / I take now / will make a big difference / in the future.

절약하는 습관

🗣️ 스피킹1_ 중요 패턴 익히기

It shows me exactly <u>where my money goes.</u>
의문사(구) + 주어 + 동사

- I don't know <u>where my phone is</u>. It was on the table earlier.

- I'm not sure <u>what time the meeting starts</u>. Can you check the schedule for me?

- I have no idea <u>who that person is</u>. Do you happen to know?

 **4강** 절약하는 습관

🗣 **스피킹2_ 내 이야기해 봅시다**

Q How do you usually save money?

A ▪ I save money by using public transportation during the week. I can spend less on gas and parking fees.

▪ I bring my own lunch instead of buying it. It's much cheaper.

▪ I make a budget every month and try to spend within it.

▪ Actually, I'm not very good at saving, so sometimes I end up overspending.

4강 절약하는 습관

👁 본문 [해석]

<나는 어떻게 절약하는가>

돈을 절약하는 습관을 들이는 것은 내가 미래를 위해 할 수 있는 최고의 일 중 하나라고 생각해요. 저축은 단순히 돈을 더 많이 가지는 것뿐만 아니라, 안전하고 안정된 느낌을 주기도 하죠. 저는 매일 조금씩 아끼기 위해 커피를 직접 가져가거나 집에서 음식을 만들어 먹는 것 같은 작은 변화를 시도해요. 그리고 월 예산을 세우는 것도 도움이 되는데, 이렇게 하면 돈이 어디로 쓰이는지 정확히 알 수 있어서 더 똑똑하게 선택할 수 있거든요. 이런 식으로 하면 자동차 수리나 의료비 같은 예상치 못한 지출이 생기더라도 스트레스를 받지 않고 대비가 되죠. 지금 이런 작은 걸음들이 앞으로 큰 변화를 만들어 줄 거라고 믿어요.

4강 절약하는 습관

🗣 스피킹1_ 중요 패턴 익히기 [해석]

It shows me exactly <u>where my money goes.</u>

: (간접의문문) 의문사 + 주어 + 동사

- 내 전화기가 어디 있는지 모르겠어. 아까는 테이블 위에 있었어.

- 회의가 몇 시에 시작하는지 확실하지 않아. 일정 좀 확인해 줄래?

- 저 사람이 누군지 전혀 모르겠어. 혹시 알고 있어?

🗣 스피킹2_ 내 이야기해 봅시다 [해석]

질문 보통 어떻게 돈을 절약하나요?

답
- 저는 평일에 대중교통을 이용해서 돈을 절약해요. 그래서 기름값과 주차비를 덜 쓰게 돼요.

- 저는 점심을 사 먹는 대신 직접 싸 가요. 그게 훨씬 저렴해요.

- 매달 예산을 세우고 그 안에서 소비하려고 노력해요.

- 사실 저는 돈을 잘 아끼지 못해서 가끔 과소비를 하기도 해요.

 **5강** 집안일 – 요리와 청소

👁 **본문 눈으로 이해하기**

Jinsu : Hey, Alice! How often do you cook?

Alice : I try to cook dinner about three or four times a week. Cooking at home saves money and is usually healthier. How about you?

Jinsu : I cook maybe once or twice a week. I'm not a great cook, so I prefer simple meals. I eat out or order food most of the time.

Alice : That makes sense! Do you also clean regularly?

Jinsu : I try to clean my place every weekend. I like to start the week fresh. How about you?

Alice : I clean a little every day, so it doesn't get too messy. It's easier for me that way.

Jinsu : Sounds like a good plan! Maybe I'll try that, too.

5강 집안일 – 요리와 청소

👄 본문 소리 내어 읽기

Jinsu : Hey, Alice! How often do you cook?

Alice : I try to cook dinner / about three or four times a week.

Cooking at home saves money / and is usually healthier.

How about you?

Jinsu : I cook maybe once or twice a week. I'm not a great cook,

/ so I prefer simple meals. I eat out / or order food /

most of the time.

Alice : That makes sense! Do you also clean regularly?

Jinsu : I try to clean my place / every weekend. I like to start

the week fresh. How about you?

Alice : I clean a little every day, / so it doesn't get too messy.

It's easier for me / that way.

Jinsu : Sounds like a good plan! Maybe I'll try that, too.

5강 집안일 – 요리와 청소

👄 **스피킹1_ 중요 패턴 익히기**

I'm not a great cook, **so** I prefer simple meals.
: 내가 ~을 잘하지 않아서,

- I'm not a good singer, so I don't usually sing in front of others.

- I'm not a good driver, so I avoid driving long distances.

- She's a great athlete, so she's good at every sport.

5강 집안일 – 요리와 청소

👄 **스피킹2_ 내 이야기해 봅시다**

Q **How often do you cook?**

A ▪ I cook almost every day. I enjoy making my own meals.

▪ I hardly cook. I usually eat out before coming home.

▪ My husband and I both work late, so we often order food.

▪ My wife mostly cooks, and I'm in charge of the dishes.

집안일 – 요리와 청소

◎ 본문 [해석]

Jinsu : 안녕, 앨리스! 요리는 얼마나 자주 해?

Alice : 일주일에 서너 번 저녁을 만들어 보려고 노력해. 집에서 요리하면 돈도 절약되고 보통 더 건강하거든. 너는 어때?

Jinsu : 나는 일주일에 한두 번 정도 요리해. 요리를 잘하는 편은 아니라서 간단한 음식을 선호해. 대부분 외식하거나 음식을 주문해.

Alice : 그럴 수 있지! 청소도 자주 해?

Jinsu : 매주 주말마다 집을 청소하려고 해. 새롭게 한 주를 시작하는 게 좋거든. 너는?

Alice : 나는 매일 조금씩 청소해. 그래야 너무 지저분해지지 않아서 나한테는 그게 더 쉬워.

Jinsu : 정말 좋다! 달리기 이벤트가 있으면 알려줘.

Alice : 좋은 방법인 것 같아! 나도 한 번 그렇게 해봐야겠다.

집안일 – 요리와 청소

🗣 스피킹1_ 중요 패턴 익히기 [해석]

I'm not a great cook, so I prefer simple meals.
: 내가 ~을 잘하지 않아서,

- 저는 노래를 잘 부르지 못해서 보통 다른 사람들 앞에서 노래하지 않아요.

- 저는 운전을 잘하지 못해서 장거리는 운전을 피해요.

- 그녀는 훌륭한 운동선수라서 모든 스포츠를 잘해요.

🗣 스피킹2_ 내 이야기해 봅시다 [해석]

질문 얼마나 자주 요리하세요?

답
- 저는 거의 매일 요리해요. 직접 요리하는 것을 즐깁니다.

- 저는 거의 요리하지 않아요. 보통 집에 오기 전에 외식을 해요.

- 저희 남편과 저는 둘 다 늦게까지 일해서 자주 음식을 시켜 먹어요.

- 제 아내가 주로 요리하고, 저는 설거지를 맡아요.

6강 한국의 봄

◉ 본문 눈으로 이해하기

Spring in Korea usually starts in March and lasts until May. The weather becomes warmer, and the cold winter finally ends. Flowers, especially cherry blossoms, bloom all over the country in spring. It's a popular season for picnics, hikes, and outdoor festivals. Many people go outside to enjoy the beautiful flowers and fresh air.

Spring can be windy, and some days have yellow dust from China. People often wear lighter clothes, but the mornings and evenings can still be chilly. It is a transitional season, with big temperature swings between day and night, so you should be mindful of your health. Carrying a light jacket is a good idea to stay comfortable throughout the day.

👄 **본문 소리 내어 읽기**

Spring in Korea / usually starts in March / and lasts until May. The weather becomes warmer, / and the cold winter finally ends. Flowers, / especially cherry blossoms, / bloom all over the country / in spring. It's a popular season / for picnics, hikes, and outdoor festivals. Many people go outside / to enjoy the beautiful flowers / and fresh air.

Spring can be windy, / and some days have yellow dust / from China. People often wear lighter clothes, / but the mornings and evenings / can still be chilly. It is a transitional season, / with big temperature swings / between day and night, / so you should be mindful of your health. Carrying a light jacket / is a good idea / to stay comfortable / throughout the day.

6강 한국의 봄

👄 **스피킹1_ 중요 패턴 익히기**

You should be mindful of your health
: ~에 신경 써야 해, 유의해야 해

- You should be mindful of your words around kids. Try to use positive language.

- You should be mindful of others' feelings. Otherwise, you might hurt someone.

- You should be mindful of what you eat. Try to avoid eating too much sugar or salt.

6강 한국의 봄

🫦 **스피킹2_ 내 이야기해 봅시다**

Q **How do you like spring in Korea?**

A ■ I get cold easily, so I like spring because it's warm.

■ I like spring because it feels like everything is starting fresh.

■ I don't really like spring because I'm allergic to pollen. Every spring, I get a runny nose and itchy eyes.

6강 한국의 봄

◉ 본문 [해석]

한국의 봄은 보통 3월에 시작해서 5월까지 지속됩니다. 날씨가 따뜻해지며 긴 겨울이 마침내 끝이 납니다. 봄에는 특히 벚꽃이 전국 곳곳에서 피어나죠. 이 시기는 소풍, 등산, 야외 축제 등으로 인기가 많습니다. 많은 사람들이 아름다운 꽃과 신선한 공기를 즐기기 위해 밖으로 나갑니다. 봄에는 바람이 불고 가끔 중국에서 날아오는 황사가 있는 날도 있습니다. 사람들은 가벼운 옷을 입지만 아침과 저녁은 여전히 쌀쌀할 수 있습니다. 낮과 밤의 온도 차이가 큰 전환기라 건강에 신경을 쓰는 것이 좋습니다. 하루 종일 편안하게 지내기 위해 가벼운 재킷을 가지고 다니는 것이 좋은 방법입니다.

👄 스피킹1_ 중요 패턴 익히기 [해석]

You should be mindful of your health
: ~에 신경 써야 해, 유의해야 해

- 아이들 주변에서는 말을 조심해야 해요. 긍정적인 언어를 사용하도록 노력하세요.

- 다른 사람들의 감정을 신경 써야 해요. 그렇지 않으면 누군가에게 상처를 줄 수도 있어요.

- 먹는 것에 신경을 써야 해요. 설탕이나 소금을 너무 많이 먹지 않도록 해 보세요.

👄 스피킹2_ 내 이야기해 봅시다 [해석]

질문 한국의 봄은 어떠세요?

답
- 저는 추위를 잘 타서 따뜻한 봄이 좋아요.

- 봄이 모든 것이 새롭게 시작되는 느낌이 들어서 좋아요.

- 저는 꽃가루 알레르기가 있어서 봄을 그다지 좋아하지 않아요. 봄마다 콧물이 나고 눈이 가려워요.

7강 출퇴근

👁 **본문 눈으로 이해하기**

Jinsu : Hey, Alice. You told me that you're learning Korean at Yonsei University. How do you get there?

Alice : I take the bus. I'm lucky because there's a bus stop near my place. The bus goes directly to the university. It's so convenient!

Jinsu : That sounds nice. How long does it take?

Alice : About 20 minutes if there's no traffic. But sometimes it takes longer during rush hour. How about you?

Jinsu : I take the subway. I live near Sadang Station, so I take Line 4 first. Then I transfer to Line 9 at Dongjak Station. After I get off at Yeouido Station, I walk to my office.

Alice : Sounds like a long commute. How long does it take in total?

Jinsu : About 50 minutes, door to door. It's not that far in Seoul.

7강 출퇴근

🗨️ 본문 소리 내어 읽기

Jinsu : Hey, Alice. You told me **/** that you're learning Korean **/** at Yonsei University. How do you get there?

Alice : I take the bus. I'm lucky **/** because there's a bus stop **/** near my place. The bus goes directly **/** to the university. It's so convenient!

Jinsu : That sounds nice. How long does it take?

Alice : About 20 minutes **/** if there's no traffic. But sometimes **/** it takes longer during rush hour. How about you?

Jinsu : I take the subway. I live near Sadang Station, **/** so I take Line 4 first. Then I transfer to Line 9 **/** at Dongjak Station. After I get off at Yeouido Station, **/** I walk to my office.

Alice : Sounds like a long commute. How long does it take **/** in total?

Jinsu : About 50 minutes, **/** door to door. It's not that far in Seoul.

7강 출퇴근

🗣 스피킹1_ 중요 패턴 익히기

How long does it take to 동사 : ~하는 데 얼마나 걸리나요?

- How long does it take to get to Incheon Airport?

  → It takes about an hour by subway from Hongdae.

- How long does it take to fly from Incheon to New York?

  → It takes about 14 hours. It's a long flight.

👄 **스피킹2_ 내 이야기해 봅시다**

Q How do you get to work/school/the airport?

A ▪ I drive to work. It takes about half an hour.

▪ I live close to my school, so I just walk there.

▪ I work from home, so I don't have to commute.

▪ I take the airport bus to Incheon Airport.

출퇴근

◉ 본문 [해석]

Jinsu : 안녕, 앨리스. 네가 연세대학교에서 한국어를 배우고 있다고 했지.
거기까지 어떻게 가?

Alice : 난 버스를 타. 우리 집 근처에 버스 정류장이 있어서 운이 좋아.
그 버스는 대학교까지 바로 가. 정말 편리해!

Jinsu : 좋다! 시간은 얼마나 걸려?

Alice : 차가 막히지 않으면 약 20분 정도 걸려. 하지만 러시아워 때는 더
오래 걸릴 때도 있어. 너는?

Jinsu : 난 지하철을 타. 나는 사당역 근처에 살아서 먼저 4호선을 타.
그리고 동작역에서 9호선으로 갈아타. 여의도역에서 내린 후 회사
까지 걸어가.

Alice : 통근 시간이 꽤 길 것 같은데. 총 얼마나 걸려?

Jinsu : 집에서 회사까지 약 50분 정도 걸려. 서울에서는 그렇게 먼 편이 아
니야.

7강 출퇴근

😙 **스피킹1_ 중요 패턴 익히기 [해석]**

> **How long does it take to 동사 : ~하는 데 얼마나 걸리나요?**

- 인천공항까지 가는 데 얼마나 걸리나요?

  ➡ 홍대에서 지하철로 약 1시간 걸려요.

- 인천에서 뉴욕까지 비행기로 얼마나 걸리나요?

  ➡ 약 14시간 걸려요. 긴 비행이에요.

😙 **스피킹2_ 내 이야기해 봅시다 [해석]**

질문 직장/학교/공항까지 어떻게 가나요?

답
- 저는 차로 출근해요. 약 30분 걸려요.

- 저는 학교와 가까이 살아서 그냥 걸어가요.

- 저는 재택근무를 해서 출퇴근할 필요가 없어요.

- 저는 인천공항까지 공항버스를 타고 가요.

8강 호텔 시설 이용

Let me give you some details about your stay. Breakfast is available in the main dining area on the first floor every day from 7:00 a.m. to 10:30 a.m.

We have a fitness center located on the second floor, which is open 24 hours a day for your convenience. If you're interested in relaxation, the spa on the third floor offers massages and other treatments, which you can book anytime. Our pool is open from 8:00 a.m. to 9:00 p.m. and is located just past the lobby.

If you need help or have any questions, please call the front desk by pressing "0" on your room phone. We hope you enjoy your stay with us!

🫦 본문 소리 내어 읽기

Let me give you some details / about your stay. Breakfast is available / in the main dining area / on the first floor / every day from 7:00 a.m. to 10:30 a.m.

We have a fitness center / located on the second floor, / which is open 24 hours a day / for your convenience. If you're interested in relaxation, / the spa on the third floor / offers massages / and other treatments, / which you can book anytime. Our pool is open / from 8:00 a.m. to 9:00 p.m. / and is located / just past the lobby.

If you need help / or have any questions, / please call the front desk / by pressing "0" on your room phone. We hope / you enjoy your stay with us!

8강 호텔 시설 이용

👄 **스피킹1_ 중요 패턴 익히기**

Let me give you ~ : 당신에게 ~를 드릴게요

- You must be tired. Let me give you a ride.

- Let me give you a hand. It'll be faster if we do it together.

- To help you understand better, let me give you an example.

- Let me give you this book. I think you'll enjoy it.

8강 호텔 시설 이용

👄 **스피킹2_ 내 이야기해 봅시다**

Q What services do you use most often when you stay at a hotel?

A ■ I like to enjoy breakfast at the hotel restaurant.

■ I usually use room service for meals.

■ I enjoy using the pool/the fitness center/the sauna.

■ I mostly call the front desk for extra towels/pillows /hangers.

8강 호텔 시설 이용

◎ 본문 [해석]

여러분의 머무르시는 것에 대해 몇 가지 세부 사항 안내해 드리겠습니다. 아침 식사는 매일 오전 7시부터 오전 10시 30분까지 1층 메인 다이닝 구역에서 제공됩니다. 2층에 위치한 피트니스 센터가 있는데, 편의를 위해 24시간 내내 엽니다. 휴식을 원하신다면, 3층 스파에서 마사지와 기타 트리트먼트를 예약하실 수 있습니다. 스파는 언제든 예약 가능합니다. 수영장은 로비를 지나 바로 위치해 있으며, 오전 8시부터 오후 9시까지 운영됩니다.

도움이 필요하시거나 질문이 있으시면 객실 전화로 '0'번을 눌러 프런트 데스크에 연락해 주세요. 저희 호텔에서 즐거운 시간을 보내시길 바랍니다!

호텔 시설 이용

👄 **스피킹1_ 중요 패턴 익히기 [해석]**

Let me give you ~ : 당신에게 ~를 드릴게요

- 많이 피곤하시겠어요. 제가 차로 데려다 드릴게요.

- 제가 도와드릴게요. 같이 하면 더 빠를 거예요.

- 더 잘 이해할 수 있도록 예를 하나 들어 드릴게요.

- 이 책을 드릴게요. 즐겁게 읽으실 것 같아요.

👄 **스피킹2_ 내 이야기해 봅시다 [해석]**

질문 호텔에 머무를 때 어떤 서비스들을 가장 사주 이용하나요?

답
- 저는 호텔 레스토랑에서 아침 식사를 즐기는 걸 좋아해요.

- 저는 보통 식사를 룸서비스로 해결해요.

- 저는 수영장/피트니스 센터/사우나를 이용하는 것을 즐겨요.

- 저는 주로 프런트 데스크에 전화해서 추가 수건/베개/옷걸이

  를 요청해요.

9강 건강관리 - 수면, 식단

👁 **본문 눈으로 이해하기**

Jinsu : Hi Alice! How are you?

Alice : Hi Jinsu! I'm good, thanks. How about you?

Jinsu : I'm okay, but I don't think I'm sleeping enough these days.

Alice : Oh, that's not good. How many hours do you sleep at night?

Jinsu : Maybe five hours? I know it's not enough, but I'm so busy.

Alice : You should try to sleep at least seven hours. Otherwise, it might weaken your immunity.

Jinsu : You're right. I'll try. What about you? Do you sleep well?

Alice : I do. I also care about my diet. I try to eat more fresh vegetables and less junk food.

Jinsu : That's great. Do you take vitamins, too?

Alice : Of course, I take a multivitamin every day.

👄 본문 소리 내어 읽기

Jinsu : Hi Alice! How are you?

Alice : Hi Jinsu! I'm good, thanks. How about you?

Jinsu : I'm okay, but I don't think / I'm sleeping enough these days.

Alice : Oh, that's not good. How many hours / do you sleep / at night?

Jinsu : Maybe five hours? I know it's not enough, / but I'm so busy.

Alice : You should try to sleep / at least seven hours. Otherwise, / it might weaken your immunity.

Jinsu : You're right. I'll try. What about you? Do you sleep well?

Alice : I do. I also care about my diet. I try to eat more fresh vegetables / and less junk food.

Jinsu : That's great. Do you take vitamins, too?

Alice : Of course, I take a multivitamin every day.

9강 건강관리 – 수면, 식단

👄 **스피킹1_ 중요 패턴 익히기**

You should try to 동사원형 : ~하려고 노력하는 게 좋을 것 같아

- You should try to eat healthier meals. You are what you eat!

- You should try to spend more time with your family. Nothing is more important than your loved ones.

- You should try to exercise regularly. Health becomes more important as you age.

👄 **스피킹2_ 내 이야기해 봅시다**

Q How many hours do you sleep at night?

A
- I sleep around 8 hours and I feel well-rested.

- I don't sleep much, maybe 5 hours. I'm always short on sleep.

- It depends. Sometimes I stay up late, and other times I go to bed early.

- As I get older, I sleep less and wake up often.

9강 건강관리 – 수면, 식단

👁 본문 [해석]

Jinsu : 안녕, 앨리스! 잘 지내?

Alice : 안녕, 진수! 잘 지내, 고마워. 너는 어때?

Jinsu : 괜찮아, 그런데 요즘 잠을 충분히 못 자는 것 같아.

Alice : 아, 그건 좋지 않네. 밤에 몇 시간 정도 자?

Jinsu : 아마 다섯 시간쯤? 충분하지 않은 거 알지만, 너무 바빠서 그래.

Alice : 적어도 일곱 시간은 자려고 노력해야 해. 그렇지 않으면 면역력이 약해질 수도 있어.

Jinsu : 맞아, 노력해 볼게. 너는 어때? 잠 잘 자?

Alice : 응, 잘 자. 그리고 식단에도 신경 써. 신선한 채소를 더 먹으려고 하고, 정크푸드는 덜 먹으려고 해.

Jinsu : 멋지다. 비타민도 챙겨 먹어?

Alice : 당연하지. 나는 매일 멀티비타민을 먹어.

🫦 스피킹1_ 중요 패턴 익히기 [해석]

You should try to 동사원형 : ~하려고 노력하는 게 좋을 것 같아

- 더 건강한 식사를 하도록 노력해야 해요. "먹는 것이 곧 당신이에요!"

- 가족과 더 많은 시간을 보내도록 노력해야 해요. 사랑하는 사람들보다 더 중요한 건 없어요.

- 규칙적으로 운동하도록 노력해야 해요. 나이가 들수록 건강이 더 중요해져요.

🫦 스피킹2_ 내 이야기해 봅시다 [해석]

질문 밤에 몇 시간이나 자나요?

답
- 저는 약 8시간 정도 자고, 충분히 쉰 느낌이에요.

- 저는 많이 못 자요. 아마 5시간 정도? 항상 잠이 부족해요.

- 그때그때 달라요. 가끔 늦게까지 깨어 있기도 하고, 가끔은 일찍 잠자리에 들어요.

- 나이가 들수록 잠이 줄고, 자주 깨게 돼요.

 **10강** 한국의 여름

👁 **본문 눈으로 이해하기**

Summer in Korea is hot and humid. It lasts from June to August. Temperatures often rise above 30°C, (thirty degrees Celsius) and the rainy season, called jangma, brings heavy rain in late June and July.

The heat and humidity can be challenging, so it's important to stay hydrated and avoid going outside when it's very hot. Many Koreans take summer vacations in late July or early August, visiting beaches, mountains, or resorts to escape the heat.

People also enjoy cooling foods like naengmyeon, cold noodles, and bingsu, shaved ice. Although the weather can be tough, summer in Korea is a lively season full of energy and activities.

 **10강** 한국의 여름

🗣 본문 소리 내어 읽기

Summer in Korea / is hot and humid. It lasts / from June to August. Temperatures often rise / above 30°C, (thirty degrees Celsius) / and the rainy season, / called jangma, / brings heavy rain / in late June and July.

The heat and humidity / can be challenging, / so it's important / to stay hydrated / and avoid going outside / when it's very hot. Many Koreans take summer vacations / in late July or early August, / visiting beaches, mountains, or resorts / to escape the heat.

People also enjoy cooling foods / like naengmyeon, cold noodles, / and bingsu, shaved ice. Although the weather can be tough, / summer in Korea is a lively season / full of energy and activities.

10강 한국의 여름

It's important to 동사원형 : ~하는 것은 중요하다

- It's important to be on time. Being late can leave a bad impression.

- It's important to respect other people's opinions. Listen carefully and try to understand their point of view.

- It's important to keep a good balance between work and rest. Without balance, you may feel stressed or burned out.

10강 한국의 여름

Q How do you like summer in Korea?

A
- Summer is my favorite season. I enjoy outdoor activities under the sun and summer sports like surfing.

- I can't handle the heat well, so summer is really tough for me. I feel like I run out of energy easily.

- I don't like cold weather, so I prefer the heat instead. Plus, I like summer because I can go on vacation.

10강 한국의 여름

👁 본문 [해석]

한국의 여름은 덥고 습합니다. 6월부터 8월까지 지속되며, 기온이 자주 30℃ 이상으로 올라갑니다. 또한 '장마'라 불리는 우기가 6월 말에서 7월 사이에 많은 비를 동반합니다.

더위와 습도가 힘들 수 있기 때문에, 수분을 충분히 섭취하고 매우 더운 시간대에는 외출을 피하는 것이 중요합니다. 많은 한국 사람들이 7월 말이나 8월 초에 여름휴가를 떠나며, 더위를 피하기 위해 해변, 산 또는 리조트를 방문합니다.

사람들은 차가운 국수인 냉면과 갈린 얼음인 빙수 같은 시원한 음식을 즐기기도 합니다. 날씨는 힘들 수 있지만, 한국의 여름은 활기차고 다양한 활동들로 가득 찬 계절입니다.

🗣 스피킹1_ 중요 패턴 익히기 [해석]

It's important to 동사원형 : ~하는 것은 중요하다

- 시간을 지키는 것이 중요해요. 늦는 것은 나쁜 인상을 줄 수 있어요.

- 다른 사람들의 의견을 존중하는 것이 중요해요.

  잘 듣고 그들의 관점을 이해하려고 노력하세요.

- 일과 휴식 사이에 균형을 잘 유지하는 것이 중요합니다. 균형이 없으면 스트레스를 받거나 번아웃 상태가 될 수 있습니다.

🗣 스피킹2_ 내 이야기해 봅시다 [해석]

질문 한국의 여름을 어떻게 생각하세요?

답
- 여름은 제가 가장 좋아하는 계절이에요. 햇볕 아래서 야외 활동을 즐기고, 서핑 같은 여름 스포츠도 좋아해요.

- 저는 더위를 잘 못 견뎌서 여름이 정말 힘들어요. 금방 지치는 것 같아요.

- 추운 날씨를 싫어해서 더운 게 차라리 나아요. 게다가 여름엔 휴가를 갈 수 있어서 좋아요.

 **11강** **지금 뭐해?**

👁 **본문 눈으로 이해하기**

Jinsu : Hey, Alice. What are you doing now?

Alice : Hi, Jinsu. I'm booking a place to stay. I'm planning to travel to Jeonju with my brother, Kevin. We want to experience staying in a traditional Korean house.

Jinsu : That sounds great! Jeonju has so much delicious food. Make sure to try different dishes while you're there!

Alice : I will, thanks for the tip! By the way, what were you doing earlier? You looked busy.

Jinsu : Oh, I was finishing up a project for school. I had to submit it by tonight, so I was a bit stressed.

Alice : That sounds tough. I hope you can rest a bit now.

Jinsu : Yeah, I'm almost done. Take care and have a great trip!

Alice : Thanks, Jinsu! Talk to you later.

11강 지금 뭐해?

👄 본문 소리 내어 읽기

Jinsu : Hey, Alice. What are you doing now?

Alice : Hi, Jinsu. I'm booking a place to stay. I'm planning to travel to Jeonju / with my brother, Kevin. We want to experience staying / in a traditional Korean house.

Jinsu : That sounds great! Jeonju has so much delicious food. Make sure to try different dishes / while you're there!

Alice : I will, / thanks for the tip! By the way, / what were you doing earlier? You looked busy.

Jinsu : Oh, I was finishing up a project for school. I had to submit it / by tonight, / so I was a bit stressed.

Alice : That sounds tough. I hope / you can rest a bit now.

Jinsu : Yeah, I'm almost done. Take care / and have a great trip!

Alice : Thanks, Jinsu! Talk to you later.

지금 뭐해?

스피킹1_ 중요 패턴 익히기

Make sure to 동사원형 : 꼭 ~해

- The restaurant is so popular. Make sure to book ahead.

- Make sure to eat well and get enough sleep. Health comes first.

- The forecast says it's going to rain. Make sure to bring an umbrella.

11강 지금 뭐해?

👄 **스피킹2_ 내 이야기해 봅시다**

Q What are you doing these days?

A
- I'm learning tennis these days. It's harder than I thought, but I'm enjoying it.

- I'm really into studying English these days. It's a bit challenging but I'm having fun.

- I recently moved, and I'm still adjusting.

- Nothing special. Just the same routine.

지금 뭐해?

👁 본문 [해석]

Jinsu : 안녕, 앨리스. 지금 뭐 하고 있어?

Alice : 안녕, 진수. 머물 곳을 예약하고 있어. 동생 케빈이랑 전주로 여행을 갈 계획이야. 우리 전통 한옥에 머물러 보려고 해.

Jinsu : 정말 좋겠다! 전주는 맛있는 음식이 정말 많아. 거기 있는 동안 다양한 음식을 꼭 먹어 봐!

Alice : 그럴게, 조언 고마워! 그런데, 아까 뭐 하고 있었어? 바빠 보이더라.

Jinsu : 아, 학교 프로젝트를 마무리하고 있었어. 오늘 밤까지 제출해야 해서 조금 스트레스 받았어.

Alice : 힘들었겠다. 이제 좀 쉴 수 있으면 좋겠다.

Jinsu : 응, 거의 다 끝났어. 몸 조심하고 좋은 여행 되길 바래!

Alice : 고마워, 진수! 나중에 얘기하자.

11강 지금 뭐해?

🫦 **스피킹1_ 중요 패턴 익히기 [해석]**

Make sure to 동사원형 : 꼭 ~해

- 그 레스토랑은 정말 인기 있어요. 미리 예약하는 걸 꼭 잊지 마세요.

- 먹고, 충분히 자는 걸 꼭 챙기세요. 건강이 최우선이에요.

- 일기예보에 따르면 비가 올 거라고 해요. 우산을 꼭 챙기세요.

🫦 **스피킹2_ 내 이야기해 봅시다 [해석]**

질문 요즘 뭐 하며 지내세요?

답
- 요즘 테니스를 배우고 있어요. 생각보다 어렵지만, 재미있게 하고 있어요.

- 요즘 영어 공부에 푹 빠져 있어요. 조금 어렵지만, 재미있어요.

- 최근에 이사해서 아직 적응 중이에요.

- 특별한 건 없어요. 그냥 평소와 같은 일상이에요.

◉ 본문 **눈으로 이해하기**

Black Friday is a famous shopping day in the United States. It happens every year on the Friday after Thanksgiving, which is in late November. On this day, stores offer big discounts on many items, like electronics, clothes, and toys. Many people wake up early to go shopping, and some even wait in long lines before the stores open. Online shopping is also very popular on Black Friday. It's a great time to buy gifts for Christmas or things you need at a lower price. In recent years, Black Friday sales have also become popular in other countries, including South Korea.

Many online stores and malls in Korea hold special sales during this time. If you use this sale period well, you can buy good-quality items at very low prices.

12강 블랙프라이데이

👄 본문 소리 내어 읽기

Black Friday is a famous shopping day / in the United States. It happens every year / on the Friday after Thanksgiving, / which is in late November. On this day, / stores offer big discounts / on many items, / like electronics, clothes, and toys. Many people wake up early / to go shopping, / and some even wait in long lines / before the stores open. Online shopping is also very popular / on Black Friday. It's a great time to buy gifts / for Christmas / or things you need / at a lower price. In recent years, / Black Friday sales have also become popular / in other countries, / including South Korea. Many online stores and malls in Korea / hold special sales / during this time. If you use this sale period well, / you can buy good-quality items / at very low prices.

블랙프라이데이

👄 스피킹1_ 중요 패턴 익히기

It's a great time to 동사원형 : ~할 멋진 시간이다

- It's a great time to shop for winter clothes. If you shop now, you can find great deals.

- It's a great time to try something new. Whether it's a hobby or a skill, how about learning something new?

- It's a great time to catch up with friends. How about reaching out to your friends first?

👄 **스피킹2_ 내 이야기해 봅시다**

Q **Do you shop online often? What do you usually buy?**

A ■ Yes, I shop online all the time. I usually buy clothes and electronics.

■ Yes, especially during sales. I often buy cosmetics online.

■ Not really. I prefer to shop in stores, so I can see the items before buying.

12강 블랙프라이데이

👁 본문 [해석]

블랙프라이데이는 미국에서 유명한 쇼핑 날입니다. 매년 11월 말 추수감사절 다음 날 금요일에 열립니다. 이 날에는 전자제품, 의류, 장난감과 같은 다양한 품목에 대해 큰 폭의 할인을 제공합니다. 많은 사람들이 쇼핑을 하기 위해 일찍 일어나며, 일부는 매장이 열기 전에 긴 줄을 서기도 합니다. 블랙프라이데이에는 온라인 쇼핑도 매우 인기가 많습니다. 이 날은 크리스마스 선물이나 필요한 물건을 저렴한 가격에 구매하기 좋은 시기입니다. 최근 몇 년간 블랙프라이데이 세일은 한국을 포함한 다른 나라에서도 인기를 얻고 있습니다. 한국에서도 많은 온라인 스토어와 쇼핑몰이 이 시기에 특별 세일을 진행합니다. 이 세일 기간을 잘 활용하면 질 좋은 물건을 매우 저렴하게 살 수 있습니다.

12강 블랙프라이데이

👄 스피킹1_ 중요 패턴 익히기 [해석]

It's a great time to 동사원형 : ~할 멋진 시간이다

- 지금은 겨울옷을 사기에 좋은 시기예요. 지금 쇼핑하면 좋은 할인 혜택을 찾을 수 있어요.

- 지금은 새로운 것을 시도하기에 좋은 시간이에요. 취미든 기술이든 새로운 것을 배워보는 게 어때요?

- 지금은 친구들과 밀린 이야기를 나누기에 좋은 시기예요. 먼저 친구들에게 연락해 보는 건 어때요?

👄 스피킹2_ 내 이야기해 봅시다 [해석]

질문 당신은 온라인 쇼핑을 자주 하나요? 주로 무엇을 사나요?

답
- 네, 저는 항상 온라인 쇼핑을 해요. 주로 옷과 전자제품을 사요.

- 네, 특히 세일 기간이에요. 저는 주로 화장품을 온라인에서 사요.

- 딱히 그렇진 않아요. 저는 물건을 사기 전에 직접 볼 수 있도록 매장에서 쇼핑하는 것을 더 선호해요.

 **13강**

수영/운전할 수 있나요?

◉ **본문 눈으로 이해하기**

Alice : Hi, Jinsu! Can you swim?

Jinsu : No, I can't. I've never learned how to swim properly. I always feel nervous in deep water. What about you?

Alice : Yes, I can swim pretty well. I actually learned when I was a kid, and now I swim regularly. It's one of my favorite hobbies.

Jinsu : That's amazing! I wish I could swim well. It seems so cool.

Alice : It's really fun. Maybe you can take some lessons or I can help you if you want!

Jinsu : Thanks, Alice. It'll be great. By the way, can you drive?

Alice : Of course. I started driving when I was 16, but I don't drive here in Korea. What about you?

Jinsu : I can drive, but I'm not very good. I get nervous when I have to park in tight spaces.

Alice : That's totally normal! Driving takes practice, just like swimming. The more you practice, the better you become.

수영/운전할 수 있나요?

👄 본문 소리 내어 읽기

Alice : Hi, Jinsu! Can you swim?

Jinsu : No, I can't. I've never learned **/** how to swim properly.
I always feel nervous **/** in deep water. What about you?

Alice : Yes, I can swim pretty well. I actually learned **/** when
I was a kid, **/** and now I swim regularly. It's one of my
favorite hobbies.

Jinsu : That's amazing! I wish I could swim well. It seems so
cool.

Alice : It's really fun. Maybe you can take some lessons **/** or I
can help you **/** if you want!

Jinsu : Thanks, Alice. It'll be great. By the way, **/** can you drive?

Alice : Of course. I started driving **/** when I was 16, **/** but I don't
drive **/** here in Korea. What about you?

Jinsu : I can drive, **/** but I'm not very good. I get nervous **/** when
I have to park **/** in tight spaces.

Alice : That's totally normal! Driving takes practice, **/** just like
swimming. The more you practice, **/** the better you
become.

13강 수영/운전할 수 있나요?

👄 **스피킹1_ 중요 패턴 익히기**

Maybe you can 동사 : ~해 볼 수도 있지

- Maybe you can talk to your boss about the problem. He will give you some good advice.

- I know you're having a hard time. Maybe you can ask your parents for help.

- Maybe you can take an English class. I can recommend a good class for you.

13강 수영/운전할 수 있나요?

🗣 **스피킹2_ 내 이야기해 봅시다**

Q **Can you drive? If so, are you a good driver?**

A
- Yes, I can. I think I'm a good driver. I've been driving for almost 20 years without any accidents.

- I can drive, but I'm not a good driver. I try to avoid long distance or night driving.

- I have a driver's license, but I've never driven a car.

- I don't have a driver's license yet, but I want to get it soon.

13강 수영/운전할 수 있나요?

◉ 본문 [해석]

Alice : 안녕, 진수! 수영할 줄 알아?

Jinsu : 아니, 못해. 제대로 배운 적이 없어. 깊은 물에서는 항상 긴장돼. 너는 어때?

Alice : 응, 나는 수영을 꽤 잘해. 사실 어릴 때 배웠고, 지금도 정기적으로 수영해. 내가 가장 좋아하는 취미 중 하나야.

Jinsu : 정말 놀랍다! 나도 수영을 잘할 수 있으면 좋겠어. 멋져 보이네.

Alice : 정말 재미있어. 레슨을 받아보거나 원하면 내가 도와줄 수도 있어!

Jinsu : 고마워, 앨리스. 정말 좋겠다. 그런데 너 운전할 줄 알아?

Alice : 물론이지. 나는 16살 때 운전을 시작했어. 하지만 여기 한국에서는 운전을 안 해. 너는?

Jinsu : 나는 운전할 수는 있는데, 그렇게 잘하지는 않아. 좁은 공간에 주차해야 할 때 긴장돼.

Alice : 그거 완전히 정상적인 거야! 운전은 연습이 필요해. 수영처럼 말이야. 연습을 많이 할수록 더 잘하게 돼.

13강 수영/운전할 수 있나요?

👄 스피킹1_ 중요 패턴 익히기 [해석]

Maybe you can 동사 : ~해 볼 수도 있지

- 문제에 대해 상사와 이야기해 보는 게 어때요? 그분이 좋은 조언을 해 줄 거예요.

- 네가 힘든 시간을 보내고 있다는 걸 알아. 부모님께 도움을 요청해 보는 게 어때?

- 영어 수업을 들어 보는 게 어때요? 내가 좋은 수업을 추천해줄 수 있어요.

👄 스피킹2_ 내 이야기해 봅시다 [해석]

질문 운전할 줄 알아요? 그렇다면, 운선을 잘아나요?

답
- 네, 운전할 줄 알아요. 제가 운전을 잘한다고 생각해요. 사고 없이 거의 20년 동안 운전해 왔어요.

- 네, 운전할 줄은 알아요. 하지만 잘하지는 못해요. 저는 장거리 운전이나 야간 운전을 피하려고 노력해요.

- 저는 운전면허는 있지만, 차를 운전해 본 적은 없어요.

- 저는 아직 운전면허가 없지만, 곧 따고 싶어요.

 **14강** 한국의 가을

Autumn in Korea is a beautiful and meaningful season that usually lasts from September to November. The weather is cool and dry at first, but it becomes colder as the season goes on. The temperature difference between day and night is large, so it's easy to catch a cold if you're not careful. The sky is often clear and blue, and the air feels fresh. One of the most beautiful sights in autumn is the colorful leaves, called danpung in Korean. Trees turn red, orange, and yellow, and many people visit parks or mountains to enjoy the scenery. Autumn is also the time for Chuseok, a Korean harvest holiday similar to Thanksgiving. Families gather to honor their ancestors by holding memorial rituals, called jesa. They prepare special food and spend time together. Autumn in Korea is not only about the beauty of nature but also a season of rich harvest and celebration.

14강 한국의 가을

👄 **본문 소리 내어 읽기**

Autumn in Korea / is a beautiful and meaningful season / that usually lasts from September to November. The weather is cool and dry at first, / but it becomes colder / as the season goes on. The temperature difference / between day and night is large, / so it's easy to catch a cold / if you're not careful. The sky is often clear and blue, / and the air feels fresh.

One of the most beautiful sights in autumn / is the colorful leaves, / called danpung in Korean. Trees turn red, orange, and yellow, / and many people visit parks or mountains / to enjoy the scenery. Autumn is also the time for Chuseok, / a Korean harvest holiday / similar to Thanksgiving. Families gather / to honor their ancestors / by holding memorial rituals, / called jesa. They prepare special food / and spend time together. Autumn in Korea / is not only about the beauty of nature / but also a season of rich harvest and celebration.

14강 한국의 가을

🗣 스피킹1_ 중요 패턴 익히기

One of the 최상급 + 복수명사 : 가장 ~한 것들 중 하나

- She is one of the most popular singers in Korea. I love

  her unique voice and beautiful lyrics.

- This is one of the best movies that I've ever seen.

  The story was so touching, and the acting was incredible.

- One of the richest people in the world is Warren Buffet.

  He is famous for his successful investment skills.

14강 한국의 가을

👄 **스피킹2_ 내 이야기해 봅시다**

Q What's your favorite thing about autumn?

A
- Autumn is my favorite season. I enjoy hiking in the mountains to see danpung, the colorful autumn leaves.

- I like autumn because the cool and crisp air makes me feel refreshed. It's the perfect season for reading.

- Actually, I'm not a big fan of autumn. It gets colder and the days get shorter. I feel a bit gloomy during this season.

14강 한국의 가을

◎ **본문 [해석]**

한국의 가을은 아름답고 의미 있는 계절로, 보통 9월에서 11월까지 지속됩니다. 날씨는 처음에는 선선하고 건조하지만, 계절이 지나면서 점점 더 추워집니다. 낮과 밤의 기온 차가 커서 조심하지 않으면 감기에 걸리기 쉽습니다. 하늘은 보통 맑고 파란색이며, 공기는 상쾌합니다. 가을의 가장 아름다운 광경 중 하나는 단풍이라고 불리는 색색의 나뭇잎들입니다. 나무들은 빨강, 주황, 노랑으로 물들고, 많은 사람들이 공원이나 산을 방문해 그 경치를 즐깁니다. 가을은 또한 추석의 계절이기도 합니다. 추석은 추수감사절과 비슷한 한국의 추수 명절입니다. 가족들은 모여 제사라고 불리는 조상을 기리는 의식을 지냅니다. 그들은 특별한 음식을 준비하고 함께 시간을 보냅니다. 한국의 가을은 단지 자연의 아름다움만 있는 계절이 아니라, 풍성한 수확과 축하의 계절이기도 합니다.

스피킹1_ 중요 패턴 익히기 [해석]

One of the 최상급 + 복수명사 : 가장 ~한 것들 중 하나

- 그녀는 한국에서 가장 인기 있는 가수들 중 한 명이다. 나는 그녀의 독특한 목소리와 아름다운 가사를 좋아한다.

- 이것은 내가 본 최고의 영화들 중 하나이다. 이야기는 매우 감동적이었고, 연기는 놀라웠다.

- 세계에서 가장 부유한 사람들 중 한 명은 워런 버핏이다. 그는 성공적인 투자 실력으로 유명하다.

스피킹2_ 내 이야기해 봅시다 [해석]

질문   가을에 대해 가장 좋아하는 것은 무엇인가요?

답
- 가을은 제가 가장 좋아하는 계절이에요. 저는 산에 가서 알록달록한 단풍을 보는 하이킹을 즐깁니다.

- 저는 가을을 좋아해요. 선선하고 상쾌한 공기가 저를 기분 좋게 만들어 줘요. 이 계절은 독서하기에 완벽한 때라고 생각해요.

- 사실 저는 가을을 그렇게 좋아하지 않아요. 날씨가 추워지고, 낮이 짧아지거든요. 이 계절 동안 저는 조금 우울해지는 것 같아요.

15강 해외식당 전화예약

◉ **본문 눈으로 이해하기**

Staff : Hello, thank you for calling [Outback Steakhouse]. How may I help you?

Customer : Hi, I'd like to make a reservation for four people.

Staff : Sure. When would you like to come in?

Customer : Tomorrow evening at 7 p.m., if possible.

Staff : I'm sorry, but we're fully booked at that time. How about 6 p.m.?

Customer : Oh, I'm afraid I can't make it at that time. Is 8 p.m. available?

Staff : Let me check. Yes, 8 p.m. is available. May I know your name, please?

Customer : Yes, it's Minsu Lee.

Staff : Thank you, Mr. Lee. Could you spell your name, please?

Customer : Sure, it's M-I-N-S-U, L-E-E. M as in Mary, I as in Ice cream, N as in Nancy, S as in Sam, U as in Umbrella, L as in Lion, E as in Elephant, E as in Elephant.

Staff : Got it, thank you. Your table for four at 8 p.m. tomorrow is confirmed under Minsu Lee. Anything else I can help you with?

Customer : No, thank you. That's all.

Staff : My pleasure. Have a great day! We'll see you tomorrow.

👄 본문 소리 내어 읽기

Staff : Hello, thank you for calling [Outback Steakhouse].
How may I help you?

Customer : Hi, I'd like to make a reservation / for four people.

Staff : Sure. When would you like to come in?

Customer : Tomorrow evening at 7 p.m., / if possible.

Staff : I'm sorry, / but we're fully booked / at that time.
How about 6 p.m.?

Customer : Oh, I'm afraid / I can't make it / at that time. Is 8 p.m.
available?

Staff : Let me check. Yes, 8 p.m. is available. May I know
your name, please?

Customer : Yes, it's Minsu Lee.

Staff : Thank you, Mr. Lee. Could you spell your name,
please?

Customer : Sure, it's M-I-N-S-U, L-E-E. M as in Mary, / I as in
Ice cream, / N as in Nancy, / S as in Sam, / U as in
Umbrella, / L as in Lion, / E as in Elephant, / E as in
Elephant.

Staff : Got it, thank you. Your table for four / at 8 p.m.
tomorrow / is confirmed / under Minsu Lee. Anything
else / I can help you with?

Customer : No, thank you. That's all.

Staff : My pleasure. Have a great day! We'll see you tomorrow.

해외식당 전화예약

👄 스피킹1_ 중요 패턴 익히기

May I 동사원형? : 제가 ~해도 될까요?

- May I sit here?

  → Sure, go ahead. ↔ Sorry, but this seat is taken.

  → Feel free to. ↔ I'm afraid not. I'm waiting for someone.

- May I borrow your pen?

  → Sure, here you are. ↔ I'm sorry but I need it right now.

  → Of course. No problem. ↔ I wish I could. I don't have one.

- May I have your attention, please? Let me begin my presentation.

👄 **스피킹2_ 내 이야기해 봅시다**

A May I know your name, please?

B Yes, it's Jenna Kim.

A Could you spell your name, please?

B Sure, it's J-E-N-N-A, K-I-M. J as in John, E as in Elephant, N as in Nancy, N as in Nancy, A as in Apple, K as in Kite, I as in Ice cream, M as in Mary.

자주 쓰이는 알파벳별 대표 단어

A: Apple	H: House	O: Orange	V: Victor
B: Boy	I: Ice cream	P: Peter	W: Water
C: Cat	J: John	Q: Queen	X: X-ray
D: Dog	K: Kite	R: Rabbit	Y: Yellow
E: Elephant	L: Lion	S: Sam	Z: Zebra
F: Frank	M: Mary	T: Tiger	
G: George	N: Nancy	U:Umbrella	

해외식당 전화예약

👁 본문 [해석]

직원 : 안녕하세요, [아웃백 스테이크하우스]에 전화 주셔서 감사합니다. 어떻게 도와드릴까요?

손님 : 안녕하세요, 네 명 예약을 하고 싶습니다.

직원 : 물론입니다. 언제 오실 건가요?

손님 : 가능하다면 내일 저녁 7시예요.

직원 : 죄송하지만, 그 시간에는 이미 예약이 다 찼습니다. 6시는 어떠세요?

손님 : 아, 그 시간에는 어려울 것 같아요. 8시는 가능할까요?

직원 : 확인해 보겠습니다. 네, 8시는 가능합니다. 성함을 여쭤봐도 될까요?

손님 : 네, 민수 이입니다.

직원 : 감사합니다, 이 씨. 이름 철자를 말씀해 주실 수 있나요?

손님 : 물론이죠. M-I-N-S-U, L-E-E입니다. M은 Mary의 M, I는 Ice cream의 I, N은 Nancy의 N, S는 Sam의 S, U는 Umbrella의 U, L은 Lion의 L, E는 Elephant의 E, E는 Elephant의 E입니다.

직원 : 확인했습니다. 감사합니다. 내일 저녁 8시에 네 분 예약이 Minsu Lee 이름으로 확인되었습니다. 더 도와드릴 일이 있을까요?

손님 : 아니요, 감사합니다. 이걸로 충분해요.

직원 : 도와드릴 수 있어서 기쁩니다. 좋은 하루 보내세요! 내일 뵙겠습니다.

🗣 스피킹1_ 중요 패턴 익히기 [해석]

May I 동사원형? : 제가 ~해도 될까요?

- 여기 앉아도 될까요?
  - ➜ 네, 그러세요. ⟷ 죄송하지만, 이 자리는 다른 누구 거예요.
  - ➜ 편하게 그러세요. ⟷ 죄송하지만 안 될 것 같네요. 제가 누군가를 기다리고 있어요.
- 펜 좀 빌려도 될까요?
  - ➜ 물론이죠, 여기 있어요. ⟷ 죄송하지만, 제가 지금 필요해서요.
  - ➜ 물론이에요, 문제없어요. ⟷ 빌려드리고 싶은데, 펜이 없네요.
- 주목해 주시겠어요? 제가 발표 시작하겠습니다.

🗣 스피킹2_ 내 이야기해 봅시다 [해석]

A 성함을 여쭤봐도 될까요?

B 네, 제 이름은 Jenna Kim입니다.

A 이름 철자를 말씀해 주실 수 있을까요?

B 물론이죠. J-E-N-N-A, K-I-M입니다.J는 John의 J, E는 Elephant 의 E, N은 Nancy의 N, N은 Nancy의 N, A는 Apple의 A, K는 Kite 의 K, I는 Ice cream의 I, M은 Mary의 M입니다.

◉ **본문 눈으로 이해하기**

I have been raising a dog for ten years. It's a poodle, and its name is Choco because its fur is chocolate-colored. Having a dog has many advantages. First, Choco gives me emotional comfort. Whenever I feel sad or stressed, he comforts me and makes me feel better. Second, I never feel lonely because Choco is always with me, no matter what happens.

However, raising a dog also has some challenges. When Choco gets sick, the medical bills can be expensive. Traveling can be tricky because I have to find someone to take care of him while I'm away. Owning a pet requires not only responsibility but also sacrifice.

Before Choco, I had another dog who passed away due to old age, and it was a very painful experience. I was so heartbroken that it took me a long time to recover. But now, Choco is my loyal companion. He is not just a pet; he is my family. I hope Choco stays healthy and lives with me for a long time.

👄 **본문 소리 내어 읽기**

I have been raising a dog / for ten years. It's a poodle, / and its name is Choco / because its fur is chocolate-colored. Having a dog has many advantages. First, / Choco gives me emotional comfort. Whenever I feel sad or stressed, / he comforts me / and makes me feel better. Second, / I never feel lonely / because Choco is always with me, / no matter what happens.

However, / raising a dog also has some challenges. When Choco gets sick, / the medical bills can be expensive. Traveling can be tricky / because I have to find someone / to take care of him / while I'm away. Owning a pet requires / not only responsibility / but also sacrifice.

Before Choco, / I had another dog / who passed away due to old age, / and it was a very painful experience. I was so heartbroken / that it took me a long time / to recover. But now, / Choco is my loyal companion. He is not just a pet; he is my family. I hope / Choco stays healthy / and lives with me / for a long time.

🐾 스피킹1_ 중요 패턴 익히기

so A(형용사/부사) that B(주어+동사) : 너무 A해서(원인) B하다(결과)

- It was such a busy day. I was so tired that I just passed out.

- The movie was so funny that I couldn't stop laughing.

  I highly recommend it.

- It snowed heavily last night and the road was so slippery that we had to drive very slowly.

🗣 스피킹2_ 내 이야기해 봅시다

Q Have you ever raised any pets?

A
- Yes, I've raised a dog. Her name was Momo, and she was a Maltese. We used to go for a walk every evening. I miss her.

- Yes, I have a cat right now. You should meet him. He's so cute and smart.

- No, I haven't. I'm allergic to animal fur, but my children want to have a pet, so I'm not sure what to do.

👁 **본문 [해석]**

나는 강아지를 10년째 키우고 있다. 그것은 푸들이고, 이름은 초코이다. 초코라는 이름은 털 색깔이 초콜릿 색이라 붙여졌다. 강아지를 키우는 것에는 많은 장점이 있다.

첫째, 초코는 나에게 정서적인 위안을 준다. 내가 슬프거나 스트레스를 받을 때마다 초코는 나를 위로하고 기분을 좋게 만들어 준다. 둘째, 초코는 항상 내 곁에 있어서 나는 절대 외로움을 느끼지 않는다. 무슨 일이 생기더라도.

하지만 강아지를 키우는 데에는 어려움도 있다. 초코가 아플 때, 병원비가 많이 들 수 있다. 그리고 여행을 가는 것도 까다로울 수 있는데, 내가 없는 동안 초코를 돌봐 줄 사람을 찾아야 하기 때문이다. 반려동물을 키우는 것은 책임감뿐 아니라 희생도 요구한다.

초코 이전에, 나는 다른 강아지를 키웠었는데, 그 강아지는 노령으로 인해 세상을 떠났다. 그것은 정말 고통스러운 경험이었다. 나는 너무 슬퍼서 회복하는 데 오랜 시간이 걸렸다. 하지만 지금 초코는 나의 충실한 동반자이다. 그는 단순한 반려동물이 아니라 나의 가족이다. 나는 초코가 건강하게 오래 내 곁에서 살아주기를 바란다.

16강 반려동물

스피킹1_ 중요 패턴 익히기 [해석]

> **so A(형용사/부사) that B(주어+동사) : 너무 A해서(원인) B하다(결과)**

- 정말 바쁜 하루였다. 나는 너무 피곤해서 그냥 뻗어 버렸다.

- 그 영화가 너무 재미있어서 웃음을 멈출 수 없었다. 나는 그 영화를 강력히 추천한다.

- 어젯밤에 눈이 많이 내렸고, 길이 너무 미끄러워서 우리는 천천히 운전해야 했다.

🗣 **스피킹2_ 내 이야기해 봅시다 [해석]**

질문 반려동물을 키워본 적 있나요?

답
- 네, 저는 강아지를 키워본 적이 있어요. 그녀의 이름은 모모였고, 몰티즈였어요. 우리는 매일 저녁 산책을 하곤 했어요. 그녀가 그리워요.

- 네, 지금 고양이를 키우고 있어요. 한번 만나 보세요. 정말 귀엽고 똑똑해요.

- 아니요, 저는 반려동물을 키워본 적이 없어요. 동물 털 알레르기가 있어서요. 하지만 제 아이들은 반려동물을 키우고 싶어 해서 어떻게 해야 할지 고민이에요.

17강 운동 권유

◉ 본문 눈으로 이해하기

Alice : Hi, Jinsu!! How have you been?

Jinsu : Hi Alice. I've been really busy these days. I don't have much free time.

Alice : Really? Why?

Jinsu : Well, I work during the day, and at night, I go to graduate school. So, I have so much to do.

Alice : Wow, you must be really tired! But do you exercise at all?

Jinsu : Not really. I'm too busy, so I don't have time to exercise. Actually, I feel like I'm losing energy these days. I get tired so easily.

Alice : Oh no, that's not good! If you work a lot but don't exercise, your health will get worse.

Jinsu : I know... but it's really hard to make time for it.

Alice : That's why you should start with something simple. How about this weekend? Let's go hiking together!

Jinsu : Hiking? Hmm, I haven't done that in ages.

Alice : Hiking is good for both cardio and strength training.

Jinsu : That sounds nice. Okay, let's give it a try.

Alice : Great! I'll help you stay healthy. You'll thank me later!

본문 소리 내어 읽기

Alice : Hi, Jinsu! How have you been?

Jinsu : Hi Alice. I've been really busy these days. I don't have much free time.

Alice : Really? Why?

Jinsu : Well, I work during the day, **/** and at night, **/** I go to graduate school. So, I have so much to do.

Alice : Wow, you must be really tired! But do you exercise at all?

Jinsu : Not really. I'm too busy, **/** so I don't have time to exercise. Actually, **/** I feel like **/** I'm losing energy these days. I get tired so easily.

Alice : Oh no, that's not good! If you work a lot but don't exercise, **/** your health will get worse.

Jinsu : I know... but it's really hard **/** to make time for it.

Alice : That's why you should start with something simple. How about this weekend? Let's go hiking together!

Jinsu : Hiking? Hmm, I haven't done that **/** in ages.

Alice : Hiking is good **/** for both cardio and strength training.

Jinsu : That sounds nice. Okay, let's give it a try.

Alice : Great! I'll help you stay healthy. You'll thank me later!

I feel like 주어 + 동사 : ~인 것 같은 기분이 들어

- I feel like I'm catching a cold. I don't feel well. I need to go see a doctor.

- I feel like it's going to rain soon. We should hurry and wrap it up.

- I feel like we've met before. You look familiar. Do I know you?

17강 운동 권유

👄 **스피킹2_ 내 이야기해 봅시다**

Q **Do you exercise? If so, what kind of exercise do you do?**

A ■ I do. I go to the gym three times a week, and I go hiking every weekend.

■ Yes, I take a long walk every day, and I play golf once a week.

■ Sure, I take yoga classes twice a week, and I ride my exercise bike at home.

■ Not really. I know I have to, but it's hard to make time for exercise.

17강 운동 권유

◎ 본문 [해석]

Alice : 안녕, 진수! 잘 지냈어?

Jinsu : 안녕, 앨리스. 요즘 정말 바빴어. 자유 시간이 거의 없어.

Alice : 정말? 왜?

Jinsu : 음, 낮에는 일하고 밤에는 대학원에 다니거든. 그래서 할 일이 정말 많아.

Alice : 와, 정말 피곤하겠다! 그런데 운동은 조금이라도 해?

Jinsu : 거의 안 해. 너무 바빠서 운동할 시간이 없어.

　　　　사실 요즘 에너지가 떨어지는 것 같아. 너무 쉽게 피곤해져.

Alice : 어, 그거 안 좋은데!

　　　　일은 많이 하는데 운동을 안 하면 건강이 나빠질 거야.

Jinsu : 알지... 하지만 시간 내기가 정말 어려워.

Alice : 그래서 간단한 것부터 시작하는 게 좋지.

　　　　이번 주말 어때? 같이 등산 가자!

Jinsu : 등산? 음, 정말 오랫동안 안 해 봤는데.

Alice : 등산은 유산소 운동과 근력 운동 모두에 좋아.

Jinsu : 괜찮네. 좋아, 한번 해 볼게.

Alice : 잘됐다! 내가 네 건강 관리를 도와줄게. 나중에 나한테 고마워할 걸!

17강 운동 권유

👄 스피킹1_ 중요 패턴 익히기 [해석]

I feel like 주어 + 동사 : ~인 것 같은 기분이 들어

- 감기에 걸리는 것 같아. 몸이 좀 안 좋아. 병원에 가봐야겠어.

- 곧 비가 올 것 같아. 서둘러서 마무리해야겠어.

- 우리 전에 만난 적 있는 것 같아. 낯이 익은데, 내가 너를 아나? (우리
  아는 사이야?)

👄 스피킹2_ 내 이야기해 봅시다 [해석]

질문 운동하시나요? 그렇다면, 어떤 종류의 운동을 하세요?

답
- 네, 해요. 일주일에 세 번 헬스장에 가고, 주말마다 등산을 가요.

- 네, 매일 긴 산책을 하고, 일주일에 한 번 골프를 쳐요.

- 물론이죠. 일주일에 두 번 요가 수업을 듣고, 집에서 실내 자전
  거를 타요.

- 거의 안 해요. 운동해야 한다는 건 알지만, 시간을 내기가 어려
  워요.

18강 한국의 겨울

👁 **본문 눈으로 이해하기**

Winter in Korea is very cold. It usually starts in December and lasts until February. Temperatures can drop below -10 degrees Celsius, so people wear puffer jackets and thermal underwear. Hand warmers, often called "hot packs" in Korea, are very popular winter items to stay warm.

Snow often falls in winter, and the roads can freeze, so drivers need to be very careful to avoid accidents. Many people go skiing and snowboarding at ski resorts, and children enjoy sledding when the snow piles up.

Korean schools have a two-month winter vacation in January and February. During this time, students travel with their families or take extra classes. Also, many schools hold graduation ceremonies in winter.

Winter is also the time for Korea's traditional holiday, Seollal, or Lunar New Year. Families gather to honor their ancestors through a traditional ceremony, called jesa. After the ceremony, they enjoy a special meal together, including tteokguk (rice cake soup), which symbolizes growing one year older.

👄 **본문 소리 내어 읽기**

Winter in Korea is very cold. It usually starts in December / and lasts until February. Temperatures can drop / below -10 degrees Celsius, / so people wear puffer jackets / and thermal underwear. Hand warmers, / often called "hot packs" in Korea, / are very popular winter items / to stay warm.

Snow often falls in winter, / and the roads can freeze, / so drivers need to be very careful / to avoid accidents. Many people go skiing and snowboarding / at ski resorts, / and children enjoy sledding / when the snow piles up.

Korean schools have a two-month winter vacation / in January and February. During this time, / students travel with their families / or take extra classes. Also, / many schools hold graduation ceremonies / in winter.

Winter is also the time / for Korea's traditional holiday, Seollal, / or Lunar New Year. Families gather / to honor their ancestors / through a traditional ceremony, / called jesa. After the ceremony, / they enjoy a special meal together, / including tteokguk (rice cake soup), / which symbolizes growing one year older.

18강 한국의 겨울

🗣 스피킹1_ 중요 패턴 익히기

> **need to** 동사원형 : ~할 필요가 있다, ~해야 한다

- I need to go grocery shopping this afternoon. There's nothing to eat at home.

- I need to charge my phone. The battery is almost dead.

⊘ 의무를 나타내는 (조)동사

표현	강도	특징	예문
Must	가장 강함	매우 강한 의무감, 권위적	You must not enter this area without permission.
Have to	강함	외부 규칙에 따른 필수적 행동	I have to finish this report by tomorrow.
Need to	중간	필요성에 기반한 의무, 실질적 필요	You need to study harder if you want to pass the exam.
Should	약함	권고, 추천, 조언	You should call her and apologize.

👄 **스피킹2_ 내 이야기해 봅시다**

Q How do you like winter in Korea?

A ▪ I like winter because I love skiing and snowboarding. Every winter, I look forward to visiting ski resorts.

▪ Winter can be freezing, but I enjoy eating winter food like hotteok.

▪ I don't like winter because it's so dry, and it makes my skin itchy.

▪ I'm not a big fan of winter. I get cold easily, so I don't feel like going out this season.

👁 본문 [해석]

한국의 겨울은 매우 춥습니다. 보통 12월에 시작해서 2월까지 이어집니다. 기온이 영하 10도 이하로 떨어질 수 있어서 사람들은 패딩 재킷과 내복을 입습니다. 한국에서 흔히 핫팩이라 불리는 핸드워머(손난로)는 추위를 이기기 위한 겨울철 인기 아이템입니다.

겨울에는 눈이 자주 내리고 도로가 얼어붙을 수 있어 운전자는 사고를 피하기 위해 매우 조심해야 합니다. 많은 사람들이 스키장에 가서 스키와 스노보드를 즐기며, 아이들은 눈이 쌓이면 눈썰매를 타며 놀곤 합니다.

한국의 학교들은 1월과 2월 두 달 동안 겨울방학을 합니다. 이 기간 동안 학생들은 가족과 여행을 가거나 추가 수업을 듣습니다. 또한 많은 학교들이 겨울에 졸업식을 개최합니다.

겨울은 또한 한국의 전통 명절인 설날, 즉 음력 새해를 맞이하는 시기이기도 합니다. 가족들이 모여 제사라고 불리는 전통 의식을 통해 조상을 기립니다. 제사 후에는 떡국을 포함한 특별한 식사를 함께 즐기는데, 떡국은 한 살 더 먹는 것을 상징합니다.

18강 한국의 겨울

👄 스피킹1_ 중요 패턴 익히기 [해석]

need to 동사원형 : ~할 필요가 있다, ~해야 한다

- 오늘 오후에 장을 봐야 해요. 집에 먹을 게 하나도 없어요.

- 핸드폰을 충전해야 해요. 배터리가 거의 다 닳았어요.

✓ 의무를 나타내는 (조)동사 [해석]

표현	강도	특징	예문
Must	가장 강함	매우 강한 의무감, 권위적	허가 없이 이 구역에 들어가면 안 됩니다.
Have to	강함	외부 규칙에 따른 필수적 행동	나는 내일까지 이 보고서를 끝내야 해.
Need to	중간	필요성에 기반한 의무, 실질적 필요	시험에 합격하고 싶다면 더 열심히 공부해야 해.
Should	약함	권고, 추천, 조언	그녀에게 전화해서 사과하는 게 좋아.

18강 한국의 겨울

🗨️ 스피킹2_ 내 이야기해 봅시다 [해석]

질문 한국의 겨울은 어떤가요?

답
- 저는 스키와 스노보드를 좋아해서 겨울이 좋아요. 매 겨울 스키장을 방문하는 것을 기대합니다.

- 겨울은 아주 추울 수 있지만, 호떡 같은 겨울 음식을 먹는 것을 즐깁니다.

- 저는 겨울을 안 좋아해요. 왜냐하면 너무 건조해서 제 피부를 가렵게 만들어요.

- 저는 겨울을 그다지 좋아하지 않아요. 추위를 잘 타서 이 계절에는 밖에 나가고 싶지 않아요.

MEMO

 **19강** **10년 후 계획**

◉ 본문 눈으로 이해하기

Alice : Hey, Jinsu. What do you want to do in 10 years?

Jinsu : Hmm, I think I want to be a brand manager. Right now, I'm studying marketing in graduate school, so that's my goal.

Alice : That sounds interesting! Do you have any other personal plans?

Jinsu : Yes, personally, I want to have a family. I hope to be a good husband and a great dad someday.

Alice : That's so nice! Well, for me, I'm learning Korean now at the language school. In the future, I want to become a Korea expert.

Jinsu : Wow, that sounds great! Do you want to study more about Korea?

Alice : Yes, I've already studied about Asia in college, but I want to focus more on Korea now.

Jinsu : That's amazing. You really love Korea!

Alice : I do! But there's something else I really want to do besides studying. I want to save money and travel around Europe.

Jinsu : Europe sounds exciting. Which countries do you want to visit?

Alice : All of them, if possible! As an American, I've always dreamed of seeing Europe, but I've never been there.

Jinsu : That's a great dream, Alice. I'm sure you'll make it happen.

👄 **본문 소리 내어 읽기**

Alice : Hey, Jinsu. What do you want to do in 10 years?

Jinsu : Hmm, I think / I want to be a brand manager. Right now, / I'm studying marketing / in graduate school, / so that's my goal.

Alice : That sounds interesting! Do you have any other personal plans?

Jinsu : Yes, personally, / I want to have a family. I hope to be a good husband / and a great dad someday.

Alice : That's so nice! Well, for me, I'm learning Korean now / at the language school. In the future, / I want to become a Korea expert.

Jinsu : Wow, that sounds great! Do you want to study / more about Korea?

Alice : Yes, I've already studied about Asia / in college, but I want to focus / more on Korea now.

Jinsu : That's amazing. You really love Korea!

Alice : I do! But there's something else / I really want to do / besides studying. I want to save money / and travel around Europe.

Jinsu : Europe sounds exciting. Which countries do you want to visit?

Alice : All of them, / if possible! As an American, / I've always dreamed of seeing Europe, / but I've never been there.

Jinsu : That's a great dream, Alice. I'm sure / you'll make it happen.

19강 **10년 후 계획**

🗣 스피킹1_ 중요 패턴 익히기

I'm sure 주어 + 동사 : ~라고 확신해

- I'm sure you'll do great. Just be yourself!

- I'm sure this is the right way. But let's double-check, just in case.

- I'm sure he didn't mean to upset you. Don't take it personally.

👄 **스피킹2_ 내 이야기해 봅시다**

Q **What do you want to do in 10 years?**

A ▪ In 10 years, my children will be adults, and then I
want to travel around the world.

▪ I'll probably retire in 10 years and I want to start my
own business.

▪ I want to improve my English skills so I can make
foreign friends and talk with them.

▪ Well, I don't have any special plans. We never know
what will happen in the future.

10년 후 계획

👁 본문 [해석]

Alice : 안녕, 진수. 너는 10년 후에 무엇을 하고 싶어?

Jinsu : 음, 나는 브랜드 매니저가 되고 싶어. 지금은 대학원에서 마케팅을 공부하고 있어서, 그게 내 목표야.

Alice : 흥미롭다! 다른 개인적인 계획도 있어?

Jinsu : 응, 개인적으로는 가정을 꾸리고 싶어. 언젠가는 좋은 남편이자 훌륭한 아빠가 되고 싶어.

Alice : 정말 멋지다! 나는 지금 한국어 학당에서 한국어를 배우고 있어. 미래에는 한국 전문가가 되고 싶어.

Jinsu : 와, 멋지다! 한국에 대해 더 공부하고 싶어?

Alice : 응, 나는 이미 대학에서 아시아에 대해 공부했지만, 이제 한국에 더 집중하고 싶어.

Jinsu : 대단하다. 너 정말 한국을 좋아하는구나!

Alice : 맞아! 하지만 공부 외에 정말 하고 싶은 게 또 있어. 돈을 모아서 유럽을 여행하고 싶어.

Jinsu : 유럽이라니 정말 신난다. 어떤 나라들을 가보고 싶어?

Alice : 가능하다면 전부! 나는 미국인으로서 항상 유럽을 보고 싶다는 꿈을 꿔 왔는데, 아직 한 번도 가본 적이 없어.

Jinsu : 정말 멋진 꿈이야, 앨리스. 난 네가 꼭 이룰 거라고 확신해.

19강 10년 후 계획

👄 스피킹1_ 중요 패턴 익히기 [해석]

I'm sure 주어 + 동사 : ~라고 확신해

- 나는 네가 잘할 거라고 확신해. 그냥 너답게 해!

- 나는 이게 맞는 길이라고 확신해. 하지만 혹시 모르니 한 번 더 확인해보자.

- 그가 너를 속상하게 하려고 한 건 아니라고 확신해. 너무 개인적으로 받아들이지 마.

👄 스피킹2_ 내 이야기해 봅시다 [해석]

질문 10년 뒤에 무엇을 하고 싶나요?

답
- 10년 후에는 제 아이들이 성인이 될 것이고, 그때 세계를 여행하고 싶습니다.

- 저는 아마 10년 후에 은퇴할 것이고, 제 사업을 시작하고 싶습니다.

- 저는 영어 실력을 키워서 외국인 친구를 사귀고 그들과 대화하고 싶습니다.

- 글쎄요, 저는 특별한 계획 없어요. 미래에 뭐가 일어날지 우리는 절대 모르죠.

20강 나의 가족

👁 **본문 눈으로 이해하기**

I'm in my early 60s, and I run a small restaurant. I got married 32 years ago. My wife and I have different tastes and personalities. In the early years of our marriage, we argued a lot, but over time, we've been finding common ground.

We have two children. My oldest daughter is married and now expecting a baby. She resembles me a lot both in appearance and personality. She works as a nurse at a small hospital. My daughter and son-in-law were college sweethearts, and they got married after dating for 10 years. My son-in-law is an office worker, and I like him because he is responsible and family-oriented.

My second child, a son, is still a university student. People often say he looks like my wife. He is studying computer science and hopes to work at an IT company. We used to play football and go hiking together when he was a child. Now he is all grown up and taller than me.

I started my restaurant a decade ago after quitting my job. It was really tough in the beginning, but now I'm used to it, and thankfully, the business is doing well.

My goal is to retire in five years and travel with my wife. I want us to enjoy a peaceful and relaxing life together.

👄 **본문 소리 내어 읽기**

I'm in my early 60s, / and I run a small restaurant. I got married / 32 years ago. My wife and I have different tastes and personalities. In the early years of our marriage, / we argued a lot, / but over time, / we've been finding common ground. We have two children. My oldest daughter is married / and now expecting a baby. She resembles me a lot / both in appearance and personality. She works / as a nurse / at a small hospital. My daughter and son-in-law / were college sweethearts, / and they got married / after dating for 10 years. My son-in-law is an office worker, / and I like him / because he is responsible / and family-oriented.

My second child, / a son, / is still a university student. People often say / he looks like my wife. He is studying computer science / and hopes to work / at an IT company. We used to play football / and go hiking together / when he was a child. Now he is all grown up / and taller than me.

I started my restaurant / a decade ago / after quitting my job. It was really tough / in the beginning, / but now I'm used to it, / and thankfully, / the business is doing well.

My goal is to retire / in five years / and travel with my wife. I want us to enjoy a peaceful and relaxing life together.

20강 나의 가족

👄 **스피킹1_ 중요 패턴 익히기**

want A to 동사원형 : A가 ~하기를 원하다

- Your room is too messy. I want you to clean it yourself.

- I want you to be happy. Nothing else matters. Please take care of yourself.

- Do you want me to help you? Just let me know if you need anything.

20강 나의 가족

👄 **스피킹2_ 내 이야기해 봅시다**

Q Do you have any siblings?
= Do you have any brothers or sisters?

A ▪ Yes, I have a younger brother. I'm the oldest and he is 3 years younger than me.

▪ Yes, I have an older brother and a younger sister. I'm in the middle and we are very close.

▪ Yes, I'm from a big family. I have two sisters and two brothers. I'm the third out of five.

> 〈서수〉
> first, second, third, fourth, fifth, sixth, seventh, eighth, ninth, tenth

▪ No, I'm an only child, but I have a lot of cousins, so I never felt lonely.

20강 나의 가족

저는 60대 초반이고, 작은 식당을 운영하고 있습니다. 32년 전에 결혼했습니다. 아내와 저는 취향과 성격이 다릅니다. 결혼 초에는 자주 싸웠지만, 시간이 지나면서 서로 접점을 찾아오고 있습니다.

저희는 두 자녀가 있습니다. 첫째 딸은 결혼해서 이제 아기를 기다리고 있습니다. 그녀는 외모와 성격 모두 저를 많이 닮았습니다. 작은 병원에서 간호사로 일하고 있습니다. 딸과 사위는 대학 시절 연애를 시작해 10년을 사귄 후 결혼했습니다. 사위는 사무직에 종사하며, 책임감 있고 가족 중심적인 성격이라 제가 좋아합니다.

둘째 자녀인 아들은 아직 대학생입니다. 사람들은 그가 아내를 많이 닮았다고 말합니다. 그는 컴퓨터공학을 전공하고 있고, IT 회사에서 일하기를 희망합니다. 어렸을 때 우리는 함께 축구를 하고 등산을 하곤 했습니다. 이제 그는 다 자라 저보다 키도 큽니다.

저는 10년 전, 직장을 그만두고 식당을 시작했습니다. 처음에는 정말 힘들었지만, 지금은 적응했고, 다행히 사업이 잘되고 있습니다. 제 목표는 5년 후에 은퇴하고 아내와 함께 여행을 떠나는 것입니다. 함께 평화롭고 여유로운 삶을 즐기고 싶습니다.

나의 가족

👄 스피킹1_ 중요 패턴 익히기 [해석]

want A to 동사원형 : A가 ~하기를 원하다

- 너 방이 너무 지저분해. 네가 직접 치워줬으면 좋겠어.

- 네가 행복하길 바래. 다른 건 중요하지 않아. 스스로 잘 챙기세요.

- 내가 도와줄까? 필요한 게 있으면 말해줘.

👄 스피킹2_ 내 이야기해 봅시다 [해석]

질문 형제자매가 있나요? = 형제나 자매가 있나요?

답
- 네, 저는 동생이 하나 있어요. 저는 첫째이고, 그는 저보다 3살 어립니다.

- 네, 저는 형과 여동생이 있어요. 저는 중간이고, 우리는 정말 가까운 사이입니다.

- 네, 저는 대가족 출신이에요. 형제자매는 두 명의 자매와 두 명의 형제가 있어요. 저는 다섯 명 중 셋째입니다.

- 아니요, 저는 외동이에요. 하지만 사촌들이 많아서 외롭다고 느끼지 않았어요.

MEMO

MEMO

제나쌤의
영어리스닝
길잡이

죽어라 안들리던 영어가 드디어 들리기 시작한다!

토종 한국인 영어강사 본인과 지난 15년간
수많은 영어학습자들의 영어 귀를 트여준 검증된 학습법

#이런 분들께 이 책과 온라인강의를 추천드립니다

✦ 영어공부 나름 십수년 했는데 실력이 제자리같은 분
✦ 특히 눈으로는 대충 알겠는데, 막상 귀로 들으면 안들리는 분
✦ 리스닝이지만 리딩과 스피킹 실력도 동시에 함께 늘리고 싶은 분
✦ 나의 삶과 내가 사는 한국에 대해 영어로 어떻게 표현하는지 배우고 싶은 분

#학생들의 강의평

여지껏 영어공부는 듣기만 하고 눈으로만 했던 공부였는데, 내 입으로 말하고 녹음하니 너무 재밌었습니다. 외국인 친구에게 들려줬더니 너무 잘한다고 칭찬 받았어요. - 에*더님

소리내어 읽기가 진짜 많은 도움이 되어서 요즘 미드볼 때 소리가 블럭화되어 뇌를 밟고 지나가는 느낌으로 들려요. - 명*은 님

제나쌤 강의를 통해 습득된 영어표현이 현지에서 들리고, 배운 패턴문장을 적용하여 스피킹으로 출력하는 제 모습에 깜짝 놀랐습니다. - Five *님

직접 읽어보니 자신감도 늘고, 반복하면 할 수록 잘 읽혀지고 속도도 느는게 신기했어요. 공부하고 들으니 더 잘들렸구요. - 민*님

소리내어 읽으면 영어가 들린다

제나쌤의
영어리스닝
길잡이

나의 삶, 한국, 해외여행 편

2권

유튜브 채널 [길잡이영어]
[봄봄클래스] 강의교재

제나(김주연) 지음

전)EBS강사 제나쌤이 알려주는
효과만점 영어귀뚫기 7단계 학습법

 영어 학습 콘텐츠
유튜브 채널 [길잡이영어]

 제나쌤 온라인 강의
[봄봄클래스]

길잡이★북스

2권

제나쌤의
영어리스닝
길잡이

나의 삶, 한국,
해외여행 편

유튜브 채널 [길잡이영어]
[봄봄클래스] 강의교재

제나(김주연) 지음

길잡이★북스

CONTENTS

 **21강**

이번 주말 계획

Alice : Hi, Jinsu! Do you have any plans for this weekend?

Jinsu : Well, I'm thinking of staying home and watching a movie. How about you? Do you have something in mind?

Alice : Well, it's my first year in Korea, and I really want to see the sunrise for the New Year.

Jinsu : That sounds great! In Korea, a lot of people go to the east coast to watch the sunrise.

Alice : Really? Do you know a good place to go?

Jinsu : Yes, you should go to Jeongdongjin in Donghae. It's very famous for its sunrise views.

Alice : That sounds perfect! Thanks for the tip. I'm planning to visit the place with my brother Kevin. Do you want to join us?

Jinsu : Of course! That would be fun. I can check how to get there.

Alice : Great! I'll prepare some snacks for the trip.

Jinsu : Awesome! Let's meet early in the morning. I think the sunrise is around 7 a.m. in winter, so we need to leave really early.

Alice : Okay, let me know about the transportation. I'm so excited to see the sunrise!

Jinsu : I'll text you later with the details. This will be a great way to start the New Year!

Alice : Absolutely! Thanks so much.

21강 이번 주말 계획

👄 본문 소리 내어 읽기

Alice : Hi, Jinsu! Do you have any plans / for this weekend?

Jinsu : Well, I'm thinking of staying home / and watching a movie. How about you? Do you have something in mind?

Alice : Well, it's my first year in Korea, / and I really want to see the sunrise / for the New Year.

Jinsu : That sounds great! In Korea, / a lot of people go to the east coast / to watch the sunrise.

Alice : Really? Do you know a good place to go?

Jinsu : Yes, you should go to Jeongdongjin / in Donghae. It's very famous for its sunrise views.

Alice : That sounds perfect! Thanks for the tip. I'm planning to visit the place / with my brother Kevin. Do you want to join us?

Jinsu : Of course! That would be fun. I can check / how to get there.

Alice : Great! I'll prepare some snacks / for the trip.

Jinsu : Awesome! Let's meet / early in the morning. I think / the sunrise is around 7 a.m. in winter, / so we need to leave really early.

Alice : Okay, let me know / about the transportation. I'm so excited / to see the sunrise!

Jinsu : I'll text you later / with the details. This will be a great way / to start the New Year!

Alice : Absolutely! Thanks so much.

👄 스피킹1_ 중요 패턴 익히기

I'm thinking of 동사ing : ~할까 생각 중이다

- I'm thinking of ordering pizza for dinner, because I don't feel like cooking. I had a hard day.

- I'm thinking of changing my hairstyle, because I'm tired of my current one. Maybe I'll try a shorter style.

- I'm thinking of buying a new phone, because my current one is too slow. I'm not sure which to buy, iPhone or Galaxy.

👄 **스피킹2_ 내 이야기해 봅시다**

Q **Do you have any special plans for this weekend?**

A ■ 확정된 계획

I'm going to travel to Jeju Island.

■ 계획 중

I'm planning to travel to Jeju Island.

■ 생각 중

I'm thinking of traveling to Jeju Island.

■ I'm going to attend my nephew's wedding. I'm planning to drive there, but I think the traffic will be heavy.

■ I have a family gathering this Saturday. My mother's birthday is coming, so we're going to celebrate it.

■ Not yet. I'm just planning to organize my closet. The season is changing, so I need to put away my summer clothes.

■ Not really. I haven't thought about it. I might just rest at home and watch a movie.

이번 주말 계획

◉ 본문 [해석]

Alice : 안녕, 진수! 이번 주말에 계획 있어?

Jinsu : 음, 집에 있으면서 영화나 볼까 생각 중이야. 너는? 생각해 둔 게 있어?

Alice : 음, 내가 한국에 온 지 첫해인데, 새해를 맞이해서 일출을 보고 싶어.

Jinsu : 정말 멋지다! 한국에서는 많은 사람들이 동해안으로 가서 일출을 봐.

Alice : 정말? 좋은 장소를 알고 있어?

Jinsu : 응, 정동진에 가는 게 좋아. 일출 명소로 아주 유명해.

Alice : 완벽하다! 좋은 정보 고마워. 내 동생 케빈이랑 그곳에 갈 계획이야. 같이 갈래?

Jinsu : 물론이지! 재밌을 것 같아. 내가 어떻게 가야 하는지 알아볼게.

Alice : 좋아! 나는 여행 간식을 준비할게.

Jinsu : 멋지다! 아침 일찍 만나자. 겨울에는 일출이 오전 7시쯤이라 정말 일찍 출발해야 할 거야.

Alice : 알겠어. 교통편에 대해 알려줘. 일출을 보러 가는 게 너무 기대돼!

Jinsu : 세부 사항은 나중에 문자로 보낼게. 새해를 시작하기에 정말 멋진 방법이 될 거야!

Alice : 맞아! 정말 고마워.

이번 주말 계획

I'm thinking of 동사ing : ~할까 생각 중이다

- 저녁으로 피자를 주문할까 생각 중이에요, 요리할 기분이 아니거든요. 오늘 하루가 힘들었어요.

- 헤어스타일을 바꿀까 생각 중이에요, 지금 스타일이 지겨워서요. 아마도 더 짧은 스타일로 시도해 볼까 해요.

- 새 핸드폰을 살까 생각 중이에요, 지금 쓰는 게 너무 느려서요. 아이폰이 좋을지 갤럭시가 좋을지 아직 잘 모르겠어요.

이번 주말 계획

🗣️ **스피킹2_ 내 이야기해 봅시다 [해석]**

질문 이번 주말에 특별한 계획 있나요?

답 ■ 확정된 계획

제주도로 여행 갈 예정이에요.

■ 계획 중

제주도로 여행 갈 계획이에요.

■ 생각 중

제주도로 여행 갈까 생각 중이에요.

■ 조카 결혼식에 참석할 거예요. 운전해서 갈 계획인데, 교통이 많이 막힐 것 같아요.

■ 이번 토요일에 가족 모임이 있어요. 엄마 생신이 다가와서 함께 축하할 거예요.

■ 아직은 없어요. 그냥 옷장을 정리할까 생각 중이에요. 계절이 바뀌고 있어서 여름 옷을 정리해야 해요.

■ 별다른 계획은 없어요. 아직 생각해 보지 않았어요. 그냥 집에서 쉬면서 영화나 볼까 해요.

MEMO

 **22강** 스트레스와 정신건강

👁 **본문 눈으로 이해하기**

<How I Handle Stress and Take Care of My Mental Health>

A few years ago, when I was working at a company, I experienced extreme stress due to heavy workloads and a demanding boss. I felt so helpless and depressed that I decided to quit my job. After that, I spent a few months resting and receiving treatment to recover. That experience taught me how important mental health is.

Now, whenever I notice signs that I'm feeling down or stressed, I make an effort to take care of myself. In particular, I like to go for a walk. Moving my body clears my thoughts and gives me energy. When it feels too hard to handle, I see a doctor for counseling and sometimes get prescribed medicine. This helps to prevent things from getting worse. By using these methods, I can handle stress and stay mentally healthy. Taking care of my mind is just as important as taking care of my body.

👄 **본문 소리 내어 읽기**

<How I Handle Stress / and Take Care of My Mental Health>

A few years ago, / when I was working at a company, / I experienced extreme stress / due to heavy workloads / and a demanding boss. I felt so helpless and depressed / that I decided to quit my job. After that, / I spent a few months resting / and receiving treatment to recover. That experience taught me / how important mental health is.

Now, / whenever I notice signs / that I'm feeling down or stressed, / I make an effort / to take care of myself. In particular, / I like to go for a walk. Moving my body clears my thoughts / and gives me energy. When it feels too hard to handle, / I see a doctor for counseling / and sometimes get prescribed medicine. This helps to prevent things / from getting worse.

By using these methods, / I can handle stress / and stay mentally healthy. Taking care of my mind / is just as important as taking care of my body.

22강   스트레스와 정신건강

🗣 스피킹1_ 중요 패턴 익히기

spend A(시간/돈) + 동사ing : A를 ~하는 데 쓰다

- I spend an hour studying English every day. I take online lessons from Monday to Friday, and I read aloud the day's passage.

- I'm worried about my son. He spends too much time playing computer games. I've talked to him several times, but he doesn't listen.

- I spent almost 500 dollars eating out last month. I think I should cut back and start saving money.

 **22강** 스트레스와 정신건강

👄 **스피킹2_ 내 이야기해 봅시다**

Q How do you handle your stress?

A ▪ When I'm stressed, I enjoy eating spicy foods like maratang. It helps with minor stress, but I always end up gaining weight.

▪ When I'm stressed, I go out to exercise. For me, moving my body is the best way to relieve stress.

▪ When I'm stressed, I just sleep. The problem doesn't go away, but I feel better after sleeping. Then, I think about what to do next.

▪ When I'm stressed, I have a drink with my best friend and talk about my problem. Once I open up, I feel much better.

22강 스트레스와 정신건강

👁 본문 [해석]

<내가 스트레스를 관리하고 정신 건강을 돌보는 방법>

몇 년 전, 회사에서 일할 때, 과도한 업무량과 까다로운 상사 때문에 극심한 스트레스를 경험했다. 너무 무력하고 우울해서 결국 일을 그만두기로 결심했다. 그 후 몇 달 동안 쉬고 치료를 받으며 회복했다. 그 경험은 정신 건강이 얼마나 중요한지 깨닫게 해주었다.

이제 내가 기분이 다운되거나 스트레스를 느낀다는 신호를 알아차릴 때마다 스스로를 돌보려는 노력을 한다. 특히 나는 산책을 좋아한다. 몸을 움직이면 생각이 정리되고 에너지가 생긴다. 감당하기 힘들 때는 의사를 찾아 상담을 받고, 때로는 약을 처방받기도 한다. 이는 상황이 더 악화되는 것을 막아준다.

이런 방법들을 통해 나는 스트레스를 관리하고 정신적으로 건강을 유지할 수 있다. 마음을 돌보는 것은 몸을 돌보는 것만큼이나 중요하다.

스트레스와 정신건강

👄 스피킹1_ 중요 패턴 익히기 [해석]

spend A(시간/돈) + 동사ing : A를 ~하는 데 쓰다

- 나는 매일 한 시간씩 영어를 공부한다. 나는 월요일부터 금요일까지 온라인 수업을 듣고, 그날의 지문을 소리 내어 읽는다.

- 나는 아들이 걱정된다. 그는 컴퓨터 게임을 하는 데 너무 많은 시간을 보낸다. 몇 번이나 그와 얘기했지만, 그는 듣지 않는다.

- 나는 지난달 외식하는 데 거의 500달러를 썼다. 줄이고 돈을 아끼기 시작해야 할 것 같다.

👄 **스피킹2_ 내 이야기해 봅시다 [해석]**

질문 어떻게 스트레스를 관리하나요?

답
- 내가 스트레스를 받을 때, 나는 마라탕 같은 매운 음식을 먹는 것을 즐긴다. 작은 스트레스에는 도움이 되지만, 결국에는 항상 살이 찌게 된다.

- 내가 스트레스를 받을 때, 나는 운동하러 밖에 나간다. 내게는 몸을 움직이는 것이 스트레스를 해소하는 가장 좋은 방법이다.

- 내가 스트레스를 받을 때, 나는 그냥 잔다. 문제가 사라지지는 않지만, 자고 나면 기분이 더 나아진다. 그런 다음, 무엇을 할지 생각한다.

- 내가 스트레스를 받을 때, 나는 제일 친한 친구와 술 한 잔하며 내 문제에 대해 이야기한다. 속마음을 털어놓으면 기분이 훨씬 나아진다.

MEMO

 **23강** 새해계획 – 독서

◎ 본문 눈으로 이해하기

Alice : Hi, Jinsu! Happy New Year!

Jinsu : Happy New Year, Alice! Do you have any New Year's resolutions?

Alice : Yes! I really want to improve my Korean this year.

Jinsu : That's a great goal! Your Korean is already really good.

Alice : Thanks, but I still need to practice a lot. I'm also going to read more books in English.

Jinsu : Why English books? Isn't English your first language?

Alice : Yes, but since I moved to Korea and started learning Korean, I haven't read many books in English. I feel like my English vocabulary is getting worse!

Jinsu : I know how you feel. These days, I only read books for my major, so I feel like I don't think deeply enough.

Alice : That makes sense. Do you have any special plans this year?

Jinsu : For me, my goal is to read one book every month. I've already made a list of books that I want to read.

Alice : That sounds great. Let's read a lot this year!

Jinsu : Absolutely! Let's make it a great year!

👄 **본문** 소리 내어 읽기

Alice : Hi, Jinsu! ! Happy New Year!

Jinsu : Happy New Year, Alice! Do you have any New Year's resolutions?

Alice : Yes! I really want to improve my Korean this year.

Jinsu : That's a great goal! Your Korean is already really good.

Alice : Thanks, / but I still need to practice a lot. I'm also going to read more books / in English.

Jinsu : Why English books? Isn't English your first language?

Alice : Yes, but since I moved to Korea / and started learning Korean, / I haven't read many books in English. I feel like / my English vocabulary is getting worse!

Jinsu : I know / how you feel. These days, / I only read books / for my major, / so I feel like / I don't think deeply enough.

Alice : That makes sense. Do you have any special plans this year?

Jinsu : For me, / my goal is to read one book / every month. I've already made a list of books / that I want to read.

Alice : That sounds great. Let's read a lot this year!

Jinsu : Absolutely! Let's make it a great year!

23강 새해계획 - 독서

My goal is to 동사원형 : 내 목표는 ~하는 것이다

- My goal is to get a license as an English guide. I want to help foreign tourists experience Korean culture.

- My goal is to learn how to play the piano. I'm planning to take lessons and practice regularly.

- My goal is to spend more quality time with my family. My children are growing up so quickly, and I don't want to miss out on precious moments.

- My goal is to be more considerate and understanding. I'll try to listen more and judge less.

👄 **스피킹2_ 내 이야기해 봅시다**

Q Do you have any New Year's resolutions?

A ■ I'm motivated to study English now, so I'm going to keep studying English. I believe in the power of consistency.

■ I'm going to quit smoking. It's time to make a change, and I want to set a good example for my kids.

■ I want to travel to New Zealand. I've heard the country has amazing landscapes.

■ I want to reflect more on myself and become a better person as I get older.

23강 새해계획 - 독서

👁 본문 [해석]

Alice : 안녕, 진수! 새해 복 많이 받아!

Jinsu : 새해 복 많이 받아, 앨리스! 새해 계획 있어?

Alice : 응! 올해는 정말 내 한국어 실력을 향상시키고 싶어.

Jinsu : 좋은 목표다! 네 한국어는 이미 정말 잘하는데.

Alice : 고마워, 하지만 여전히 많이 연습해야 해. 아, 그리고 영어로 된 책
도 더 읽을 거야.

Jinsu : 왜 영어 책? 영어가 네 모국어 아니야?

Alice : 맞아, 하지만 한국으로 이사 와서 한국어 공부를 시작한 이후로 영
어 책을 많이 안 읽었어. 그래서 내 영어 어휘가 더 나빠진 것 같아!

Jinsu : 무슨 말인지 알아. 요즘은 전공 관련 책만 읽다 보니 깊이 있는 생
각을 잘 못하는 것 같아.

Alice : 그럴 수 있지. 너는 올해 특별한 계획 있어?

Jinsu : 나는 한 달에 한 권씩 책을 읽는 게 목표야. 읽고 싶은 책 목록도
이미 만들어 놨어.

Alice : 멋지다. 올해 책 많이 읽자!

Jinsu : 당연하지! 멋진 한 해 만들어 보자!

🗣 스피킹1_ 중요 패턴 익히기 [해석]

My goal is to 동사원형 : 내 목표는 ~하는 것이다

- 내 목표는 영어 가이드 자격증을 취득하는 것입니다. 외국인 관광객들이 한국 문화를 체험할 수 있도록 돕고 싶습니다.

- 내 목표는 피아노를 배우는 것입니다. 레슨을 받고 규칙적으로 연습할 계획입니다.

- 내 목표는 가족과 더 의미 있는 시간을 보내는 것입니다. 아이들이 너무 빨리 자라고 있어서 소중한 순간들을 놓치고 싶지 않습니다.

- 내 목표는 더 배려심 있고 이해심 많은 사람이 되는 것입니다. 더 많이 듣고 덜 판단하려고 노력할 것입니다.

👄 스피킹2_ 내 이야기해 봅시다 [해석]

질문 새해 결심이 있나요?

답
- 지금 영어 공부에 동기부여가 돼 있어서 계속 영어 공부를 할 계획이에요. 저는 꾸준함의 힘을 믿어요.

- 담배를 끊을 거예요. 이제 변화가 필요하고, 아이들에게 좋은 본보기를 보여 주고 싶어요.

- 뉴질랜드에 여행 가고 싶어요. 그 나라의 풍경이 정말 놀랍다는 얘기를 들었어요.

- 자신을 더 성찰하고 나이가 들수록 더 나은 사람이 되고 싶어요.

MEMO

◎ **본문 눈으로 이해하기**

I don't drink alcohol very often, but I enjoy having a drink when I'm in a good mood.

On special occasions, my wife and I like to prepare a nice dinner at home. We usually enjoy wine with steak or other fancy dishes.

In the past, Korean style company dinners were focused on heavy drinking, but things have changed. These days, we occasionally go out for dinner and have just a light drink.

Most of the time, we go to a Korean barbecue restaurant and pair the meal with soju or beer.

I can't handle alcohol well, so I get tipsy easily. I usually drink about half a bottle of soju. In Korea, we have a culture of eating anju (food paired with alcohol), and my favorite is fried chicken. Sharing chicken and beer (we call it "chimaek") with my friends or family is a small joy that means a lot to me.

I know alcohol isn't great for my health, but I think drinking in moderation can make me feel good and create a pleasant atmosphere.

24강 음주

👄 **본문 소리 내어 읽기**

I don't drink alcohol very often, **/** but I enjoy having a drink **/** when I'm in a good mood.

On special occasions, **/** my wife and I **/** like to prepare a nice dinner **/** at home. We usually enjoy wine **/** with steak or other fancy dishes.

In the past, **/** Korean style company dinners **/** were focused on heavy drinking, **/** but things have changed. These days, **/** we occasionally go out for dinner **/** and have just a light drink. Most of the time, **/** we go to a Korean barbecue restaurant **/** and pair the meal **/** with soju or beer.

I can't handle alcohol well, **/** so I get tipsy easily. I usually drink **/** about half a bottle of soju. In Korea, **/** we have a culture of eating "anju" **/** (food paired with alcohol), **/** and my favorite is fried chicken. Sharing chicken and beer **/** (we call it "chimaek") **/** with my friends or family **/** is a small joy **/** that means a lot to me.

I know **/** alcohol isn't great **/** for my health, **/** but I think **/** drinking in moderation **/** can make me feel good **/** and create a pleasant atmosphere.

24강 음주

🗣 스피킹1_ 중요 패턴 익히기

be focused on 명사/대명사/동명사 : ~에 집중하다

- I felt tired all the time, so I thought I had to do something. Now, I'm focused on staying healthy.

- I'm focused on studying English now. It's not easy, but I feel like I'm improving little by little.

- I'm focused on raising my kids right now. I miss working, but I'm happy that I can spend more time with them.

24강 음주

🗨 **스피킹2_ 내 이야기해 봅시다**

Q Do you drink? If yes, what's your favorite drink?

A
- Yes, I like beer, but I'm not a big drinker. I hate hangovers.

- Yes, I enjoy drinking soju with samgyeopsal (pork belly), but I try to drink in moderation.

- Yes, but only a little. I drink socially when I'm with friends, so I don't have any favorite drinks.

- No, I don't drink at all because it's genetic. I usually drink soda when I'm at a party with drinks. but I really enjoy eating anju (food paired with alcohol).

24강 음주

◎ **본문 [해석]**

나는 술을 자주 마시지 않지만, 기분이 좋을 때 한 잔 하는 것을 즐긴다. 특별한 날에는 아내와 내가 집에서 맛있는 저녁을 준비하곤 한다. 우리는 보통 스테이크나 다른 고급 요리에 와인을 곁들여 즐긴다.

과거에는 한국의 회식 문화가 과도한 음주에 초점이 맞춰져 있었지만, 지금은 많이 바뀌었다. 요즘 우리는 가끔 저녁 식사를 위해 외출하고 가볍게 한 잔만 마신다. 대부분의 경우, 우리는 한국식 바비큐 레스토랑에 가서 소주나 맥주와 함께 식사를 즐긴다.

나는 술을 잘 못 마셔서 쉽게 취한다. 보통 소주 반 병 정도만 마신다. 한국에서는 술과 함께 안주를 먹는 문화가 있는데, 내가 가장 좋아하는 안주는 치킨이다. 친구들이나 가족들과 함께 치킨과 맥주(우리는 이를 '치맥'이라고 부른다)를 나누는 것은 나에게 큰 의미가 있는 작은 기쁨이다. 나는 술이 건강에 좋지 않다는 것을 알지만, 적당히 마시는 것이 기분을 좋게 하고 즐거운 분위기를 만들어 준다고 생각한다.

be focused on 명사/대명사/동명사 : ~에 집중하다

- 나는 항상 피곤함을 느꼈고, 그래서 뭔가 해야겠다고 생각했다. 지금은 건강을 유지하는 데 집중하고 있다.

- 나는 지금 영어 공부에 집중하고 있다. 쉽지는 않지만 조금씩 나아지고 있다는 느낌이 든다.

- 나는 지금 아이들을 키우는 데 집중하고 있다. 일을 그리워하지만, 대신 아이들과 더 많은 시간을 보낼 수 있어 행복하다.

스피킹2_ 내 이야기해 봅시다 [해석]

질문 술을 드시나요? 그렇다면, 가장 좋아하는 술은 무엇인가요?

답
- 네, 맥주는 좋아하지만 술을 많이 마시지는 않습니다. 저는 숙취가 정말 싫어요.

- 네, 저는 삼겹살과 함께 소주를 마시는 것을 즐깁니다. 하지만 적당히 마시려고 노력해요.

- 네, 하지만 아주 조금만 마십니다. 저는 친구들과 사교적인 자리에서만 술을 마시기 때문에 특별히 좋아하는 술은 없어요.

- 아니요, 저는 전혀 술을 마시지 않아요. 유전적인 이유 때문이에요. 술자리에서는 보통 소다를 마십니다. 하지만 저는 안주(술과 함께 먹는 음식)를 정말 즐겨요.

MEMO

25강 결심과 계획 - 다이어트

👁 **본문 눈으로 이해하기**

Alice : Hi, Jinsu, are you alright? You don't look well today.

Jinsu : I'm just feeling sick. I stayed up late working on my report last night and had ramen as a late-night snack. I think I have an upset stomach.

Alice : Oh, that's not good. Did you take any medicine?

Jinsu : I did, but it's not helping. I think I need to cut down on late-night snacks. I'm gaining weight, too! I sit at my desk all day and don't exercise. It's a total disaster!

Alice : I see. It's hard to stay healthy with your schedule. But if you want to lose weight, I think you should change your snacks.

Jinsu : You're right. I've decided to lose weight this year, but it's really hard. Do you have any suggestions?

Alice : That's a great decision! For late-night snacks, try eating some protein, like boiled eggs.

Jinsu : Hmm, I see. I think I eat too many carbs, like ramen or bread. I'm going to try that from now on.

Alice : Also, don't sit down right after lunch. Try walking around, even for a few minutes.

Jinsu : Thanks, Alice. I'll do my best to change my habits!

Alice : You can do it, Jinsu! Just let me know if you need more tips. When it comes to dieting, I'm quite an expert myself.

25강 결심과 계획 – 다이어트

😙 본문 소리 내어 읽기

Alice : Hi, Jinsu, are you alright? You don't look well today.

Jinsu : I'm just feeling sick. I stayed up late **/** working on my report last night **/** and had ramen **/** as a late-night snack. I think **/** I have an upset stomach.

Alice : Oh, that's not good. Did you take any medicine?

Jinsu : I did, **/** but it's not helping. I think **/** I need to cut down on late-night snacks. I'm gaining weight, too! I sit at my desk **/** all day **/** and don't exercise. It's a total disaster!

Alice : I see. It's hard to stay healthy **/** with your schedule. But if you want to lose weight, **/** I think **/** you should change your snacks.

Jinsu : You're right. I've decided **/** to lose weight **/** this year, **/** but it's really hard. Do you have any suggestions?

Alice : That's a great decision! For late-night snacks, **/** try eating some protein, like boiled eggs.

Jinsu : Hmm, I see. I think **/** I eat too many carbs, **/** like ramen or bread. I'm going to try that from now on.

Alice : Also, don't sit down **/** right after lunch. Try walking around, **/** even for a few minutes.

Jinsu : Thanks, Alice. I'll do my best **/** to change my habits!

Alice : You can do it, Jinsu! Just let me know **/** if you need more tips. When it comes to dieting, **/** I'm quite an expert myself.

결심과 계획 – 다이어트

👄 **스피킹1_ 중요 패턴 익히기**

When it comes to 명사/동명사 : ~에 관한 한

- When it comes to fried chicken, I think that restaurant is the best. It's a little expensive, but It's worth the price.

- When it comes to cleaning, no one can beat my mother. She's very neat and tidy, and she always keeps the house spotless.

- When it comes to learning a language, consistency is the key. Over time, you'll notice your skills improve.

👄 **스피킹2_ 내 이야기해 봅시다**

Q Have you ever been on a diet?

A ▪ Yes, a few years ago, I suddenly gained weight, so I combined exercise with a diet. I ended up losing 5 kilograms.

▪ Of course, and I'm still on a diet. I'm doing intermittent fasting.I think it works the best for me.

▪ Well, I always try, but it doesn't work well. Losing weight is harder as I age.

▪ No, I haven't. I think I'm naturally slim and I'm not a big eater.

◎ **본문 [해석]**

Alice : 안녕, 진수야. 괜찮아? 오늘 안 좋아 보인다.

Jinsu : 그냥 몸이 안 좋아. 어젯밤에 보고서 작업하느라 늦게까지 깨어 있었고, 야식으로 라면을 먹었어. 속이 좀 안 좋은 것 같아.

Alice : 아, 그거 안 좋다. 약은 먹었어?

Jinsu : 먹었는데 별로 효과가 없어. 야식을 줄여야 할 것 같아. 게다가 살도 찌고 있어! 하루 종일 책상에 앉아 있고, 운동도 안 하거든. 완전히 엉망이야!

Alice : 그렇구나. 네 스케줄로는 건강 유지하기가 힘들겠다. 하지만 살을 빼고 싶다면 간식을 바꿔야 할 것 같아.

Jinsu : 맞아. 올해는 살을 빼기로 결심했는데 정말 어려워. 조언 좀 해줄래?

Alice : 정말 좋은 결심이야! 야식으로 삶은 계란 같은 단백질을 먹어보는 건 어때?

Jinsu : 음, 그렇구나. 나는 라면이나 빵처럼 탄수화물을 너무 많이 먹는 것 같아. 지금부터는 그렇게 해볼게.

Alice : 그리고 점심 먹고 바로 앉지 말고, 잠깐이라도 걸어보는 게 좋아.

Jinsu : 고마워, 앨리스. 내 습관을 바꾸려고 최선을 다할게!

Alice : 할 수 있어, 진수야! 더 조언이 필요하면 말해. 다이어트에 관한 한, 나도 꽤 전문가거든.

결심과 계획 - 다이어트

👄 스피킹1_ 중요 패턴 익히기 [해석]

When it comes to 명사/동명사 : ~에 관한 한

- 프라이드 치킨에 관해서라면, 저는 그 식당이 최고라고 생각해요. 조금 비싸긴 하지만, 그만한 가치가 있어요.

- 청소에 관해서라면, 아무도 엄마를 이길 수 없어요. 엄마는 매우 깔끔하고 정돈된 분이며, 항상 집을 티끌 하나 없이 유지하세요.

- 언어를 배우는 데 있어서는 꾸준함이 핵심입니다. 시간이 지나면, 당신의 실력이 향상되는 것을 느낄 거예요.

👄 스피킹2_ 내 이야기해 봅시다 [해석]

질문 다이어트 해 본적 있나요?

답
- 네, 몇 년 전에 갑자기 살이 쪄서 운동과 다이어트를 병행했어요. 결국 5kg을 감량했어요.

- 물론이죠, 저는 여전히 다이어트를 하고 있어요. 간헐적 단식을 하고 있는데, 제게 가장 잘 맞는 것 같아요.

- 글쎄요, 항상 시도는 하는데 잘 되지 않아요. 나이가 들수록 살 빼는 게 더 어려워요.

- 아니요, 저는 다이어트를 해 본 적이 없어요. 저는 타고나길 날씬한 체질이고, 많이 먹는 편도 아니에요.

26강 스마트폰

These days, it feels like we can't live without smartphones. I feel the same way.

I've been using a smartphone since 2015. I used to use an iPhone, but now I have a Galaxy because of the Samsung Pay app. It's really convenient! There are many other applications on my smartphone, but I actually use only a few apps in my daily life. When I commute, I use a navigation app to find the fastest route. After work, I watch various videos on YouTube or American shows on Netflix. On the other hand, I don't make or receive calls very often. When I have something to say, I usually chat with my friends or family on KakaoTalk.

I think smartphones are really useful, especially when I search for information. However, I'm afraid I might rely on my smartphone too much. I need to find a good balance in using it.

 **26강** 스마트폰

👄 **본문** 소리 내어 읽기

These days, / it feels like / we can't live / without smartphones. I feel the same way.

I've been using a smartphone / since 2015. I used to use an iPhone, / but now I have a Galaxy / because of the Samsung Pay app. It's really convenient! There are many other applications / on my smartphone, / but I actually use / only a few apps / in my daily life. When I commute, / I use a navigation app / to find the fastest route. After work, / I watch various videos / on YouTube / or American shows / on Netflix. On the other hand, / I don't make / or receive calls very often. When I have something to say, / I usually chat / with my friends or family / on KakaoTalk. I think / smartphones are really useful, / especially when I search for information. However, / I'm afraid / I might rely on my smartphone too much. I need to find a good balance / in using it.

👄 스피킹1_ 중요 패턴 익히기

I'm afraid 주어 + 동사 : ~할까 걱정이다, 염려된다

- I'm afraid I might be late. The traffic is really bad.

- I'm afraid I didn't get that. Could you say that again?

- I'm afraid I can't make it tomorrow. I have another plan.

- I'm afraid we ran out of oranges. How about apple juice?

스피킹2_ 내 이야기해 봅시다

Q Which app do you use the most?

A
- I think it's YouTube. I watch a lot of videos there every day.

- I use Samsung Pay the most. I don't carry a wallet these days and pay for everything with it.

- Absolutely KakaoTalk. I use it to chat with my friends and family every day.

- Probably Naver. I use it to read the news or search for information.

👁 **본문 [해석]**

요즘 스마트폰 없이는 살 수 없을 것 같은 느낌이 들어요. 저도 공감합니다. 저는 2015년부터 스마트폰을 사용해 왔어요. 예전에는 아이폰을 사용했는데, 지금은 삼성 페이 앱 때문에 갤럭시를 쓰고 있어요. 정말 편리해요! 제 스마트폰에는 많은 앱이 있지만, 사실 일상생활에서 몇 가지 앱만 자주 사용해요. 출퇴근할 때는 가장 빠른 길을 찾기 위해 내비게이션 앱을 사용해요. 퇴근 후에는 유튜브에서 다양한 영상을 보거나 넷플릭스에서 미국 드라마를 봐요.

반면에, 저는 전화로 통화하거나 전화를 받는 일이 많지 않아요. 무슨 말을 해야 할 때는 보통 카카오톡으로 친구들이나 가족들과 채팅을 해요. 스마트폰은 정말 유용하다고 생각해요, 특히 정보를 검색할 때요. 하지만 저는 스마트폰에 너무 의존하고 있는 것 같아서 걱정이에요. 스마트폰 사용에 있어서 좋은 균형을 찾아야겠어요.

👄 스피킹1_ 중요 패턴 익히기 [해석]

I'm afraid 주어 + 동사 : ~할까 걱정이다, 염려된다

- 죄송하지만 늦을 것 같아요. 교통이 정말 막혀요.

- 죄송하지만 잘못 들었어요. 다시 말씀해 주실 수 있나요?

- 죄송하지만 내일 안 될 것 같아요. 다른 일정이 있어요.

- 죄송하지만 오렌지가 다 떨어졌어요. 사과 주스는 어떠세요?

👄 스피킹2_ 내 이야기해 봅시다 [해석]

질문 당신이 가장 많이 사용하는 앱은 무엇인가요?

답
- 아마 유튜브일 것 같아요. 저는 매일 거기서 많은 동영상을 봐요.

- 저는 삼성 페이를 가장 많이 사용해요. 요즘은 지갑을 들고 다니지 않고 모든 걸 그것으로 결제해요.

- 당연히 카카오톡이에요. 저는 그걸 사용해서 친구나 가족과 매일 채팅해요.

- 아마 네이버일 것 같아요. 저는 그걸 사용해서 뉴스를 읽거나 정보를 검색해요.

◉ 본문 **눈으로 이해하기**

Jinsu : Wow, Alice, you look great today! I love your dress. What's the occasion?

Alice : Thanks, Jinsu! I have a part-time job as an interpreter today, so I decided to dress up.

Jinsu : Oh, I see! You usually wear casual clothes, right?

Alice : Yeah, you know me. I usually just wear a T-shirt, jeans and sneakers. How about you? Do you have a dress code at work?

Jinsu : Not a full suit, but I wear business casual and dress shoes. Especially because I often meet with clients.

Alice : That makes sense. What do you wear at home?

Jinsu : At home? Just sweatpants and a comfortable T-shirt. On the weekends, I go casual, too. How about you?

Alice : Same here! Comfort is the best when you're at home.

Jinsu : Totally agree! I only have three full suits for formal occasions, such as weddings or funerals.

Alice : I'm no different! But for women, we need to put on makeup, so there's more to think about.

Jinsu : That makes sense! As long as you look neat and tidy, that's good enough.

Alice : You can say that again!

🗣 본문 소리 내어 읽기

Jinsu : Wow, Alice, / you look great today! I love your dress. What's the occasion?

Alice : Thanks, Jinsu! I have a part-time job / as an interpreter today, so I decided to dress up.

Jinsu : Oh, I see! You usually wear casual clothes, / right?

Alice : Yeah, you know me. I usually just wear a T-shirt, / jeans / and sneakers. How about you? Do you have a dress code at work?

Jinsu : Not a full suit, but I wear business casual / and dress shoes. Especially because / I often meet with clients.

Alice : That makes sense. What do you wear at home?

Jinsu : At home? Just sweatpants / and a comfortable T-shirt. On the weekends, / I go casual, too. How about you?

Alice : Same here! Comfort is the best / when you're at home.

Jinsu : Totally agree! I only have three full suits / for formal occasions, / such as weddings or funerals.

Alice : I'm no different! But for women, / we need to put on makeup, / so there's more to think about.

Jinsu : That makes sense! As long as you look neat and tidy, / that's good enough.

Alice : You can say that again!

👄 **스피킹1_ 중요 패턴 익히기**

as long as 주어 + 동사 : (주어)가 (동사) 하는 한, 하기만 하면

- You can go out as long as you finish your homework first.

  How much have you finished?

- We can go hiking as long as it doesn't rain. Have you

  checked the weather forecast?

- I want to watch the movie as long as it's not too scary.

  Have you watched the trailer?

27강 옷차림

👄 **스피킹2_ 내 이야기해 봅시다**

Q What kind of clothes do you usually wear?

A ■ I usually wear simple and comfortable clothes like cotton shirts and loose pants. However, when I go out, I prefer to dress neatly in collared shirts and slacks.

■ I wear a suit when I have a business meeting. But I wear a T shirt and sweatpants at home.

■ I prefer to wear long skirts instead of pants because they're more comfortable.

✓ **옷차림** 더 많은 영어 **표현**

블라우스	a blouse
스웨터	a sweater
폴로 셔츠	a polo shirt
후드티	a hoodie
맨투맨	a sweatshirt
민소매티	a sleeveless top
반팔티	a short-sleeved shirt
긴팔티	a long-sleeved shirt
운동복바지	sweatpants
반바지	shorts
레깅스	leggings
잠옷	pajamas
가디건	a cardigan
재킷/점퍼	a jacket
코트	a coat
작업복	work clothes
교복	a school uniform
샌들	sandals
슬리퍼(실내용)	slippers
슬리퍼(야외용)	slides

MEMO

옷차림

👁 본문 [해석]

Jinsu : 와, 앨리스, 오늘 정말 멋져 보여! 네 원피스 정말 예쁘다. 무슨 특별한 날이야?

Alice : 고마워, 진수! 오늘 통역사로 알바가 있어서 좀 차려입었어.

Jinsu : 아, 그렇구나! 너 보통은 캐주얼한 옷 입잖아, 맞지?

Alice : 응, 나 알잖아. 보통은 그냥 티셔츠, 청바지, 운동화 정도야. 너는 어때? 회사에서 정해진 복장이 있어?

Jinsu : 완전한 정장은 아니지만, 나는 비즈니스 캐주얼(세미정장)에 정장 구두를 신어. 특히 고객을 자주 만나니까.

Alice : 그럴 만하네. 집에서는 뭐 입어?

Jinsu : 집에서는? 그냥 추리닝 바지랑 편한 티셔츠. 주말에도 캐주얼하게 입어. 너는?

Alice : 나도 똑같아! 집에서는 편안함이 최고지.

Jinsu : 완전 동의해! 나는 정식 정장을 딱 세 벌만 가지고 있어. 결혼식이나 장례식 같은 공식적인 자리용으로.

Alice : 나도 별반 다르지 않아! 하지만 여자들은 화장을 해야 해서 더 신경 쓸 게 많아.

Jinsu : 이해돼! 깔끔하고 단정하게만 보이면 충분하지.

Alice : 내 말이!

옷차림

💋 **스피킹1_ 중요 패턴 익히기 [해석]**

as long as 주어 + 동사 : (주어)가 (동사) 하는 한, 하기만 하면

- 너는 숙제 끝내기만 하면 외출해도 돼. 얼마나 했어?

- 비만 오지 않으면 우리 하이킹 갈 수 있어. 일기예보 확인했어?

- 너무 무섭지만 않으면 나는 그 영화를 보고 싶어. 예고편 봤어?

💋 **스피킹2_ 내 이야기해 봅시다 [해석]**

질문 어떤 옷을 주로 입어요?

답
- 저는 보통 면 셔츠와 헐렁한 바지 같은 단순하고 편안한 옷을 입어요. 하지만 외출할 때는 칼라 있는 셔츠와 슬랙스로 단정하게 입는 것을 선호합니다.

- 저는 일 관련 미팅 때는 정장을 입습니다. 하지만 집에서는 티셔츠와 추리닝 바지를 입습니다.

- 저는 바지 대신 긴 치마를 입는 것을 선호해요. 왜냐하면 치마가 더 편하기 때문입니다.

28강 육아

I'm a mother of two young kids, and it's really challenging.
I have a 4-year-old daughter who goes to daycare and a
2-year-old son who stays home with me.

Taking care of my 2-year-old baby is a lot of work. I feed him
his meals, change diapers, give baths, and constantly keep an
eye on him because he's walking everywhere now.

When my 4-year-old daughter comes back from daycare, the
two of them at least play together for a while. That gives me
a little time to do some housework. Even so, it's exhausting.
I used to work in an office, and honestly, I think working was
easier than raising kids.

Thankfully, my husband helps out a lot. When he gets home
from work, he plays with the kids, and they love it. That's the
only time I can finally take a break.

Parenting is no joke—it's one of the hardest things I've ever
done. Raising little humans is a huge responsibility, but it's
absolutely worth it.

👄 **본문 소리 내어 읽기**

I'm a mother of two young kids, / and it's really challenging. I have a 4-year-old daughter / who goes to daycare / and a 2-year-old son / who stays home with me.

Taking care of my 2-year-old baby / is a lot of work. I feed him his meals, / change diapers, / give baths, / and constantly keep an eye on him / because he's walking / everywhere now. When my 4-year-old daughter comes back / from daycare, / the two of them / at least play together / for a while. That gives me a little time / to do some housework. Even so, / it's exhausting. I used to work in an office, / and honestly, / I think / working was easier / than raising kids.

Thankfully, / my husband helps out a lot. When he gets home / from work, / he plays with the kids, / and they love it. That's the only time / I can finally take a break. Parenting is no joke / it's one of the hardest things / I've ever done. Raising little humans / is a huge responsibility, / but it's absolutely worth it.

🗣 스피킹1_ 중요 패턴 익히기

be worth 명사/대명사/동명사 : ~할 만한 가치가 있다

- Learning English is challenging, but it's worth the effort.

- The book is worth reading. I learned so much from it.

- If you're interested in history, that spot is perfect. It's worth visiting.

- There's a long line in the restaurant, but it's worth the wait. I'm sure you won't regret it.

👄 **스피킹2_ 내 이야기해 봅시다**

Q Do you enjoy being around kids?

A ▪ Yes, I really enjoy being around kids. It's so much fun when I'm with them.

▪ Not really, I'm not very good with kids. They're cute, but I get tired after a while.

▪ Well, I didn't like kids very much, but my own child is just adorable.

▪ Yes, I do. I especially love spending time with my grandchildren. I have 2 grandsons and 1 granddaughter. They are my great joy.

◎ 본문 [해석]

저는 어린 아이 둘의 엄마이고, 정말 힘들어요. 4살 딸은 어린이집에 다니고, 2살 아들은 저와 집에 있어요. 2살 아기를 돌보는 건 정말 일이 많아요. 밥을 먹이고, 기저귀를 갈고, 목욕을 시키고, 이제 막 걸어 다니기 시작해서 항상 눈여겨봐야 해요.

4살 딸이 어린이집에서 돌아오면, 둘이 적어도 잠깐은 함께 놀아요. 그 시간이 되면 제가 조금이라도 집안일을 할 시간이 생기죠. 그래도 여전히 힘들어요. 저는 예전에 사무실에서 일했는데, 솔직히 말해서, 일하는 게 아이를 키우는 것보다 쉬웠던 것 같아요.

다행히 제 남편이 많이 도와줘요. 퇴근하고 집에 오면 아이들과 놀아주는데, 아이들이 그 시간을 정말 좋아해요. 그때가 제가 비로소 쉴 수 있는 유일한 시간이에요. 육아는 정말 만만치 않아요. 제가 해본 일 중 가장 힘든 일 중 하나예요. 아이를 키운다는 건 엄청난 책임이지만, 정말 가치 있는 일이에요.

육아

🗨 **스피킹1_ 중요 패턴 익히기 [해석]**

be worth 명사/대명사/동명사 : ~할 만한 가치가 있다

- 영어를 배우는 것은 어렵지만, 노력할 만한 가치가 있다.

- 그 책은 읽을 가치가 있다. 나는 그 책에서 많은 것을 배웠다.

- 역사에 관심이 있다면, 그 장소는 완벽해. 가볼 만한 가치가 있다.

- 그 레스토랑에 줄이 길지만, 기다릴 만한 가치가 있어. 분명 후회하지 않을 거야.

🗨 **스피킹2_ 내 이야기해 봅시다 [해석]**

질문 아이들과 함께 있는 걸 좋아하세요?

답
- 네, 저는 아이들과 함께 있는 걸 정말 좋아해요. 아이들과 함께 있으면 정말 재미있어요.

- 그다지요, 제가 아이들을 잘 다루지는 못해요. 귀엽긴 하지만, 조금 있으면 지치더라고요.

- 사실 아이들을 별로 좋아하지 않았는데, 제 아이는 정말 사랑스러워요.

- 네, 그래요. 저는 특히 제 손주들과 시간을 보내는 걸 정말 좋아해요. 손자 둘과 손녀 하나가 있는데, 그들이 제 큰 기쁨이에요.

29강 지난 주말 한 일

👁 본문 눈으로 이해하기

Jinsu : Hi Alice! Did you have a good weekend?

Alice : I did. I went to Gwangjang Market with my brother Kevin.

Jinsu : Oh, that sounds fun! What did you do there?

Alice : We ate a lot of street food like hotteok and tteokbokki. The food was so good.

Jinsu : Nice! Was it crowded?

Alice : Yes, it was super crowded. How about you? What did you do over the weekend?

Jinsu : I watched Squid Game Season 2 at home.

Alice : Oh, was it good?

Jinsu : Yes! It was so good that I only planned to watch one episode, but I ended up watching the whole season. Have you seen it?

Alice : Not yet. I don't like violent shows, so I haven't even watched Season 1 yet.

Jinsu : Ah, I see. Maybe it's not for you, then.

Alice : Yeah, probably not. But I'm glad you had fun!

🗣 본문 소리 내어 읽기

Jinsu : Alice! Did you have a good weekend?

Alice : I did. I went to Gwangjang Market / with my brother Kevin.

Jinsu : Oh, that sounds fun! What did you do there?

Alice : We ate a lot of street food / like hotteok and tteokbokki. The food was so good.

Jinsu : Nice! Was it crowded?

Alice : Yes, it was super crowded. How about you? What did you do / over the weekend?

Jinsu : I watched Squid Game Season 2 / at home.

Alice : Oh, was it good?

Jinsu : Yes! It was so good / that I only planned to watch one episode, / but I ended up watching the whole season. Have you seen it?

Alice : Not yet. I don't like violent shows, / so I haven't even watched Season 1 yet.

Jinsu : Ah, I see. Maybe it's not for you, / then.

Alice : Yeah, probably not. But I'm glad / you had fun!

스피킹1_ 중요 패턴 익히기

I'm glad 주어 + 동사 : (주어)가 (동사)해서 기뻐

- I'm glad you like it. It suits you well.

- I'm glad you came. Make yourself at home and help yourself.

- I'm glad you feel better. Take it easy and don't push yourself.

- I'm glad it worked out. I hope everything goes smoothly.

👄 **스피킹2**_ 내 이야기해 봅시다

Q How was your weekend? Did you do anything special?

A ▪ It was great. I had so much fun with my friends. We went to Busan for a trip.

▪ I spent quality time with my family at the park. It was so relaxing.

▪ Not much. I did some housework and then just relaxed at home.

▪ It wasn't great. I caught a cold and stayed in bed all weekend.

지난 주말 한 일

◉ 본문 [해석]

Jinsu : 안녕, 앨리스! 주말 잘 보냈어?

Alice : 응, 잘 보냈어. 내 남동생 케빈이랑 광장시장을 갔어.

Jinsu : 와, 재미있었겠다! 거기서 뭐 했어?

Alice : 길거리 음식 많이 먹었어. 호떡이랑 떡볶이 같은 거. 음식이 정말 맛있었어.

Jinsu : 좋다! 사람 많았어?

Alice : 응, 엄청 붐볐어. 너는 어땠어? 주말에 뭐 했어?

Jinsu : 집에서 오징어 게임 시즌 2를 봤어.

Alice : 오, 재미있었어?

Jinsu : 응! 너무 재미있어서 한 편만 보려고 했는데, 결국 시즌 전체를 다 봐버렸어. 너는 봤어?

Alice : 아직 안 봤어. 나는 잔인한 드라마를 안 좋아해서 시즌 1도 안 봤어.

Jinsu : 아, 그렇구나. 그럼 너한테는 안 맞을 수도 있겠다.

Alice : 응, 아마도 안 맞을 거야. 하지만 네가 재미있게 봤다니 다행이다.

지난 주말 한 일

🗣 스피킹1_ 중요 패턴 익히기 [해석]

I'm glad 주어 + 동사 : (주어)가 (동사)해서 기뻐

- 네가 마음에 들어 해서 기뻐. 너한테 정말 잘 어울려.

- 와줘서 기뻐. 내 집처럼 편히 지내고, 마음껏 먹어.

- 네가 나아서 다행이야. 느긋하게 하고 무리하지 마.

- 잘 돼서 기뻐. 모든 일이 순조롭게 되길 바랄게.

🗣 스피킹2_ 내 이야기해 봅시다 [해석]

질문 주말 어땠어? 뭐 특별한 거 했어?

답
- 정말 좋았어. 친구들과 정말 즐거운 시간을 보냈어. 우린 여행으로 부산에 갔어.

- 가족과 공원에서 좋은 시간을 보냈어. 정말 편안했어.

- 별거 없었어. 집안일 좀 하고 나서 그냥 집에서 쉬었어.

- 별로 좋지 않았어. 감기에 걸려서 주말 내내 침대에 있었어.

30강 지난 휴가

Last summer, my family and I went to Da Nang for our vacation. It was an amazing trip! It was a direct flight, and it took about four and a half hours. I was really excited since it was my first time flying with my family.

We stayed at a beautiful resort near the beach for five days and four nights. The weather was sunny, but during the afternoons, it got very hot. We had to stay in the water or find shade to keep cool.

My kids had so much fun playing in the pool. They especially loved the water slides and splashing around. My wife and I spent our time resting on the sunbeds by the pool. We enjoyed delicious local food and drinks. It was so peaceful and refreshing.

The vacation gave us time to relax and bond as a family. We spent meaningful time together and felt even closer as a family. I hope we can have moments like this more often.

30강 지난 휴가

👄 **본문 소리 내어 읽기**

Last summer, / my family and I went to Da Nang / for our vacation. It was an amazing trip! It was a direct flight, / and it took about four and a half hours. I was really excited / since it was my first time / flying with my family.

We stayed at a beautiful resort / near the beach / for five days and four nights. The weather was sunny, / but during the afternoons, / it got very hot. We had to stay in the water / or find shade to keep cool.

My kids had so much fun / playing in the pool. They especially loved the water slides / and splashing around. My wife and I spent our time / resting on the sunbeds / by the pool. We enjoyed delicious local food and drinks. It was so peaceful and refreshing.

The vacation gave us time / to relax and bond / as a family. We spent meaningful time together / and felt even closer / as a family. I hope / we can have moments like this / more often.

It was my first time 동사ing : ~하는 것이 처음이었다

- It was my first time traveling abroad and also my first time flying on a plane. I was excited and nervous at the same time.

- It was my first time trying Thai food. I tried Pad Thai and green curry, and I really liked them.

- It was my first time feeling so nervous. My heart was beating so fast, and my mind went completely blank.

👄 **스피킹2_ 내 이야기해 봅시다**

> **Q** **What did you do on your last vacation? Did you go somewhere nice?**

A
- Yes, I went to Jeju Island with my family. It was my third time visiting, and I enjoy it every time I go.

- Yes, I went camping in Jirisan Mountain with my friends. We had a great barbecue, enjoyed the stunning views and chatted around the campfire.

- Well, I stayed home and caught up on some sleep. Then, I watched movies and read books. It was so relaxing.

지난 휴가

◎ 본문 [해석]

지난 여름, 우리 가족은 다낭으로 휴가를 떠났습니다. 정말 멋진 여행이었어요! 직항편이었고 약 4시간 30분 정도 걸렸습니다. 가족과 함께 비행기를 탄 것이 처음이라 정말 신났습니다.

우리는 해변 근처에 있는 아름다운 리조트에서 4박 5일 동안 머물렀습니다. 날씨는 화창했지만, 오후에는 매우 더웠습니다. 더위를 식히기 위해 물속에 있거나 그늘을 찾아야 했습니다.

아이들은 수영장에서 노는 것을 정말 즐거워했어요. 특히 물 미끄럼틀과 물장난을 아주 좋아했습니다. 저와 아내는 수영장 옆 썬베드에서 쉬며 시간을 보냈습니다. 우리는 맛있는 현지 음식과 음료를 즐겼고, 정말 평화롭고 상쾌한 시간이었습니다.

이번 휴가는 우리 가족이 휴식하며 더욱 돈독해질 수 있는 시간을 주었습니다. 함께 의미 있는 시간을 보내며 가족으로서 더 가까워진 느낌이 들었습니다. 이런 시간을 더 자주 가질 수 있으면 좋겠어요.

지난 휴가

👄 스피킹1_ 중요 패턴 익히기 [해석]

It was my first time 동사ing : ~하는 것이 처음이었다

- 해외여행을 처음 가본 것이었고, 비행기를 타본 것도 처음이었어요. 설레면서도 동시에 긴장됐어요.

- 태국 음식을 처음 먹어봤어요. 팟타이와 그린 커리를 먹어봤는데, 정말 입에 잘 맞았어요.

- 그렇게 긴장한 건 처음이었어요. 심장이 너무 빠르게 뛰었고, 머리가 완전히 하얘졌어요.

👄 스피킹2_ 내 이야기해 봅시다 [해석]

질문 지난 휴가에 무엇을 하셨나요? 어디 좋은 데 가셨나요?

답
- 네, 가족과 함께 제주도에 다녀왔어요. 이번이 세 번째 방문이었는데, 갈 때마다 정말 좋아요.

- 네, 친구들과 지리산에 캠핑을 갔어요. 우리는 바비큐 파티를 하고, 멋진 경치를 즐기며 캠프파이어 옆에서 이야기를 나눴어요.

- 음, 저는 집에 머물면서 밀린 잠을 푹 잤어요. 그 후에 영화를 보고 책을 읽었는데 정말 편안했어요.

31강 나의 어린 시절

👁 **본문 눈으로 이해하기**

Alice : Hey Jinsu, where did you grow up?

Jinsu : I was born and raised in Busan. I'm a true Busan local!

Alice : Oh, that's cool. Busan is by the sea, right?

Jinsu : Yes, it is. I grew up near the beach, so seeing the ocean was just normal for me.

Alice : That sounds amazing! What were you like as a kid?

Jinsu : I was very active and outgoing just like I am now. How about you?

Alice : I was born in New York and lived there until I was 10. Then, my family moved to Chicago because of my dad's job.

Jinsu : Oh, how was that?

Alice : It was hard at first. I was really quiet and shy, so it was hard to make new friends.

Jinsu : I see. How do you like Chicago?

Alice : I like it now, but it took some time to adjust. Chicago has a lot of great food and interesting places to explore.

Jinsu : That's good to hear. I'd like to visit the city someday.

Alice : Sure! I'd be happy to show you around.

👄 **본문** 소리 내어 읽기

Alice : Hey Jinsu, / where did you grow up?

Jinsu : I was born and raised / in Busan. I'm a true Busan local!

Alice : Oh, that's cool. Busan is by the sea, / right?

Jinsu : Yes, it is. I grew up near the beach, / so seeing the ocean / was just normal for me.

Alice : That sounds amazing! What were you like / as a kid?

Jinsu : I was very active and outgoing / just like I am now. How about you?

Alice : I was born in New York / and lived there / until I was 10. Then, / my family moved to Chicago / because of my dad's job.

Jinsu : Oh, how was that?

Alice : It was hard at first. I was really quiet and shy, / so it was hard / to make new friends.

Jinsu : I see. How do you like Chicago?

Alice : I like it now, / but it took some time to adjust. Chicago has a lot of great food / and interesting places / to explore.

Jinsu : That's good to hear. I'd like to visit the city someday.

Alice : Sure! I'd be happy / to show you around.

스피킹1_ 중요 패턴 익히기

I'd be happy to 동사원형 : 기꺼이 ~할게

- I'd be happy to lend you my book. It's one of my favorite books. I think you'll enjoy it.

- I'd be happy to take care of your dog while you're away. Just let me know if you have any special instructions.

- I'd be happy to meet with you tomorrow. What time works best for you and where would you like to meet?

31강 나의 어린 시절

👄 **스피킹2_ 내 이야기해 봅시다**

Q Where did you grow up and what were you like as a kid?

A ▪ I was born and raised in Jeongseon, a small village in Gangwon-do.I was really curious and loved exploring nature.

▪ I was born in Daejeon but I grew up in Seoul during my school days. I was quiet and shy but I liked playing with other kids.

▪ I was born in Jeju and lived there until I was 13. Then I moved to Busan because of my dad's job. I was playful and energetic.

▪ I'm from Seoul. I've lived my whole life there. I was gentle and obedient as a kid.

✓ **성격을 나타내는 더 많은 표현**

- reserved (내성적인)
- cheerful (쾌활한)
- caring (자상한)
- diligent (부지런한)
- hardworking (성실한)
- lazy (게으른)
- easygoing (느긋한)
- patient (인내심 많은)
- impatient (성격이 급한)
- responsible (책임감 있는)
- serious (진지한)
- humorous (재미있는)
- friendly (상냥한, 싹싹한)
- stubborn (고집센)
- organized (계획적인)
- spontaneous (즉흥적인)
- logical (이성적인)
- empathetic (공감능력이 뛰어난)
- considerate (배려심 많은)
- rebellious (반항적인)

MEMO

나의 어린 시절

👁 본문 [해석]

Alice : 안녕 진수, 어디서 자랐어?

Jinsu : 나는 부산에서 태어나고 자랐어. 나는 진짜 부산 토박이야!

Alice : 오, 멋지네. 부산은 바다 근처지, 맞지?

Jinsu : 응, 맞아. 나는 바닷가 근처에서 자라서 바다를 보는 게 나에겐 그냥 자연스러운 일이었어.

Alice : 그거 정말 멋지다! 어렸을 때는 어떤 사람이었어?

Jinsu : 나는 지금처럼 아주 활동적이고 외향적이었어. 너는 어땠어?

Alice : 나는 뉴욕에서 태어나서 10살까지 거기서 살았어. 그 후 아버지 직장 때문에 시카고로 이사 갔어.

Jinsu : 오, 그건 어땠어?

Alice : 처음엔 힘들었어. 나는 정말 조용하고 수줍어서 새로운 친구를 사귀는 게 힘들었어.

Jinsu : 그렇구나. 시카고는 어때?

Alice : 이제는 좋아. 하지만 적응하는 데 시간이 좀 걸렸어. 시카고에는 맛있는 음식도 많고, 탐험할 곳도 많아.

Jinsu : 그거 듣기 좋다. 언젠가 그 도시에 가보고 싶어.

Alice : 물론이지! 내가 구경시켜줄게.

나의 어린 시절

🗣 스피킹1_ 중요 패턴 익히기 [해석]

I'd be happy to 동사원형 : 기꺼이 ~할게

- 나는 기꺼이 네게 내 책을 빌려줄게. 이 책은 내가 가장 좋아하는 책 중 하나야. 네가 이 책을 좋아할 것 같아.

- 나는 네가 없는 동안 네 개를 기꺼이 돌봐줄게. 특별한 지침이 있으면 알려줘.

- 나는 내일 너와 만나게 되어 기뻐. 몇 시가 가장 좋고, 어디서 만나고 싶어?

👄 **스피킹2_ 내 이야기해 봅시다 [해석]**

질문 **당신은 어디서 자랐나요? 어릴 때 어떤 아이였나요?**

답
- 나는 강원도의 작은 마을인 정선에서 태어나고 자랐다. 나는 정말 호기심이 많았고 자연을 탐험하는 것을 좋아했다.

- 나는 대전에서 태어났지만 학교 시절 동안 서울에서 자랐다. 나는 조용하고 수줍었지만 아이들과 노는 것을 좋아했다.

- 나는 제주에서 태어나 13살까지 그곳에서 살았다. 그 후 아버지 직장 때문에 부산으로 이사했다. 나는 장난기 많고 에너지가 넘쳤다.

- 나는 서울 출신이다. 평생 서울에서 살았다.
  어렸을 때 나는 얌전하고 순종적이었다.

MEMO

 **32강**

2002 월드컵

👁 **본문 눈으로 이해하기**

<My Unforgettable 2002 World Cup Experience>

I will never forget the 2002 Korea-Japan World Cup. I love soccer, so I was very happy that the World Cup was held in my country.

Korea's first match was against Poland, and we won 2:0. It was Korea's first World Cup victory ever! I cried because it was such an emotional moment. The next big match was against Italy. It was very intense. The game went into extra time, and Korea scored the winning goal to make it 2:1. The whole country went wild. When Korea beat Spain in a penalty shootout and reached the semifinals, I couldn't believe it. It felt like a dream.

In June 2002, everyone in Korea was united through soccer. People wore "Red Devils" shirts and cheered everywhere. It was like a big festival. It's one of the happiest memories of my life, and I will always treasure it.

32강 2002 월드컵

👄 **본문 소리 내어 읽기**

<My Unforgettable 2002 World Cup Experience>

I will never forget / the 2002 Korea-Japan World Cup. I love soccer, / so I was very happy / that the World Cup was held / in my country.

Korea's first match was against Poland, / and we won 2:0. It was Korea's first World Cup victory ever! I cried / because it was such an emotional moment. The next big match was against Italy. It was very intense. The game went into extra time, / and Korea scored the winning goal / to make it 2:1. The whole country went wild. When Korea beat Spain / in a penalty shootout / and reached the semifinals, / I couldn't believe it. It felt like a dream.

In June 2002, / everyone in Korea was united through soccer. People wore Red Devils shirts, / and cheered everywhere. It was like a big festival. It's one of the happiest memories of my life, / and I will always treasure it.

👄 **스피킹1_ 중요 패턴 익히기**

I will never 동사원형 : 나는 절대 ~안 할 거야

- I will never give up. I will keep trying until I make it.

- I will never forget this moment. It means a lot to me.

- I will never do that again. I promise. You can trust me

  on this.

 **32강** 2002 월드컵

👄 **스피킹2_ 내 이야기해 봅시다**

Q **What were you doing during the 2002 World Cup?**

A
- I was in high school back then. Everyone was talking about the World Cup, so it was hard to focus on studying.

- I was an office worker back then. I cheered in the streets watching the matches on a big screen. Everyone was so excited and it was really fun.

- I was living in LA at the time and watched Korea's matches with my Korean-American friends. I felt so proud because the Korean team played so well.

- I wasn't a big fan of soccer, but the 2002 World Cup was different. I think I started liking soccer from that time.

32강 2002 월드컵

👁 본문 [해석]

<나의 잊을 수 없는 2002 월드컵>

나는 2002 한일 월드컵을 절대 잊지 못할 것이다. 나는 축구를 좋아해서 월드컵이 우리나라에서 열리는 것이 정말 기뻤다.

한국의 첫 경기는 폴란드와의 경기였고, 우리는 2:0으로 이겼다. 그것은 한국의 월드컵 첫 승리였다! 나는 너무 감격적이어서 울었다. 다음 경기는 이탈리아와의 경기였다. 정말 치열한 경기였다. 경기는 연장전으로 이어졌고, 한국이 결승골을 넣어 2:1로 만들었다. 온 나라가 열광했다. 한국이 승부차기에서 스페인을 꺾고 4강에 올랐을 때, 나는 믿을 수 없었다. 꿈만 같았다.

2002년 6월은 한국의 모든 사람들이 하나가 되었던 시간이었다. 사람들은 '붉은 악마' 셔츠를 입고 어디서나 응원했다. 그것은 거대한 축제 같았다. 내 인생에서 가장 행복했던 기억 중 하나이며, 나는 그것을 항상 소중히 간직할 것이다.

32강 2002 월드컵

🗣 스피킹1_ 중요 패턴 익히기 [해석]

I will never 동사원형 : 나는 절대 ~안 할 거야

- 나는 절대 포기하지 않을 거야. 내가 해낼 때까지 계속 시도할 거야.

- 나는 이 순간을 절대 잊지 않을 거야. 이 순간은 나에게 정말 큰 의미가 있어.

- 나는 다시는 그걸 하지 않을 거야. 약속할게. 이 점에 대해서는 나를 믿어도 돼.

2002 월드컵

👄 **스피킹2_ 내 이야기해 봅시다 [해석]**

질문 2002 월드컵 하던 때 뭐하셨나요?

답

■ 나는 그때 당시 고등학생이었다. 모두가 월드컵에 대해 이야기해서 공부에 집중하기 어려웠다.

■ 나는 그때 직장인이었다. 큰 화면으로 경기를 보며 거리에서 응원했다. 모두가 너무 신나 있었고 정말 재미있었다.

■ 나는 그 당시 LA에 살고 있었고 한국계 미국인 친구들과 함께 한국 경기를 보았다. 한국 팀이 정말 잘해서 너무 자랑스러웠다.

■ 나는 축구를 별로 좋아하지 않았지만, 2002년 월드컵은 달랐다. 아마도 그때부터 축구를 좋아하게 된 것 같다.

MEMO

◎ **본문 눈으로 이해하기**

Alice : Hey, Jinsu. How were your school days?

Jinsu : Well, I was a pretty good student, but I also liked having fun with friends.How about you?

Alice : I think I was a model student. I worked hard, and always listened to my teachers. What was your favorite subject in school?

Jinsu : I liked math and science because I enjoy logical thinking. What about you?

Alice : That sounds interesting! I'm not good with numbers, so math wasn't really my thing. Instead, I loved literature and history.

Jinsu : I could tell. You liked reading and writing, didn't you?

Alice : I did. Writing essays was my favorite part of school. What subject did you not like?

Jinsu : Art! I was so bad at drawing and making things.

Alice : Really? I liked art. For me, art class was always fun and relaxing.

Jinsu : We're complete opposites! It's funny how different we are.

👄 **본문 소리 내어 읽기**

Alice : Hey, Jinsu. How were your school days?

Jinsu : Well, **/** I was a pretty good student, **/** but I also liked having fun with friends. How about you?

Alice : I think **/** I was a model student. I worked hard, **/** and always listened to my teachers. What was your favorite subject **/** in school?

Jinsu : I liked math and science **/** because I enjoy logical thinking. What about you?

Alice : That sounds interesting! I'm not good with numbers, **/** so math wasn't really my thing. Instead, **/** I loved literature and history.

Jinsu : I could tell. You liked reading and writing, **/** didn't you?

Alice : I did. Writing essays **/** was my favorite part of school. What subject did you not like?

Jinsu : Art! I was so bad at drawing **/** and making things.

Alice : Really? I liked art. For me, **/** art class was always fun and relaxing.

Jinsu : We're complete opposites! It's funny **/** how different we are.

👄 **스피킹1_ 중요 패턴 익히기**

I'm not good with 명사 : 나는 ~에 능숙하지 못해요

- I'm not good with computers. I usually ask my son for help.

- I'm not good with directions. I often get lost, even with the navigation.

- I'm not good with strangers, so it takes time to get close to new people.

- I'm not good with spicy food. I can eat it, but only a little.

33강 나의 학창시절

🫦 **스피킹2_ 내 이야기해 봅시다**

Q What was your favorite and least favorite subject in school?

A
- My favorite subject was English, and my least favorite subject was music. I was really bad at singing.
- I loved science, but I hated history. It was too much memorization.
- I liked all the subjects except math. It was too hard for me.
- Well, I didn't like studying, so lunchtime was my favorite in school.

⊘ **과목명**

과목	영어명	과목	영어명	과목	영어명
국어	Korean language	생물	biology	경제	economics
영어	English	지구과학	earth science	한문	classical Chinese
수학	mathematics (math)	사회	social studies	실과/기술가정	Home economics and Technology
과학	science	역사	history	음악	music
물리	physics	지리	geography	미술	art
화학	chemistry	도덕/윤리	ethics	체육	Physical Education (P.E.)

◉ **본문 [해석]**

Alice : 진수야, 너의 학창 시절은 어땠어?

Jinsu : 음, 나는 꽤 착한 학생이었지만, 친구들과 노는 것도 좋아했어.
　　　　 너는 어땠어?

Alice : 나는 모범생이었던 것 같아. 열심히 공부했고, 항상 선생님 말씀
　　　　 을 잘 들었지. 너는 학교에서 어떤 과목을 가장 좋아했어?

Jinsu : 나는 수학과 과학을 좋아했어. 논리적으로 생각하는 걸 즐기거든.
　　　　 너는?

Alice : 흥미롭다! 나는 숫자에 약해서 수학은 별로였어. 대신 문학과 역
　　　　 사를 정말 좋아했어.

Jinsu : 그럴 줄 알았어. 너는 독서와 글쓰기를 좋아했지, 그렇지?

Alice : 맞아. 에세이를 쓰는 게 학교에서 내가 가장 좋아하던 일이었어.
　　　　 너는 어떤 과목을 싫어했어?

Jinsu : 미술! 나는 그림 그리거나 뭔가 만드는 걸 정말 못했어.

Alice : 정말? 나는 미술을 좋아했어. 나에게 미술 시간은 항상 재미있고
　　　　 여유로운 시간이었어.

Jinsu : 우리는 완전히 반대야! 우리가 이렇게 다른 게 정말 재밌다.

나의 학창시절

👄 스피킹1_ 중요 패턴 익히기 [해석]

I'm not good with 명사 : 나는 ~에 능숙하지 못해요

- 나는 컴퓨터를 잘 다루지 못해요. 보통 아들에게 도움을 요청해요.
- 나는 길을 잘 찾지 못해요. 내비게이션을 써도 자주 길을 잃어요.
- 나는 낯선 사람들과 잘 어울리지 못해요. 그래서 새로운 사람들과 친해지는 데 시간이 걸려요.
- 나는 매운 음식을 잘 먹지 못해요. 먹을 수는 있지만 아주 조금만 가능해요.

👄 스피킹2_ 내 이야기해 봅시다 [해석]

질문 학교 다닐 때 당신이 가장 좋아한 또 가장 안 좋아한 과목은 무엇이었나요?

답
- 내가 가장 좋아했던 과목은 영어였고, 가장 싫어했던 과목은 음악이었어요. 저는 노래를 정말 못했거든요.
- 저는 과학을 좋아했지만, 역사는 싫어했어요. 외울 게 너무 많았거든요.
- 저는 수학을 제외한 모든 과목을 좋아했어요. 수학은 저에게 너무 어려웠어요.
- 글쎄요, 저는 공부하는 걸 안 좋아했어서, 학교 다닐 때 점심시간이 가장 좋았어요.

34강 잊지 못할 여행

👁 본문 눈으로 이해하기

About 20 years ago, I went on my honeymoon with my husband. We didn't want to go to a typical resort. Instead, we wanted to go somewhere special. So, we decided to go to Italy, which was full of history, art, and culture.

However, the trip didn't go as smoothly as we had imagined. In Rome, we were pickpocketed while walking on the street. We were so frustrated and ended up having a big argument that night. But afterwards, we put our heads together to figure out how to get through this situation.

At the same time, we were amazed by the famous cultural landmarks, like the Colosseum. It was breathtaking to see them in person. We also enjoyed amazing local dishes, which helped us forget about the bad experiences.

Looking back now, I can laugh about all those experiences. That honeymoon taught us how to face challenges together as a team. It was far from perfect, but it was an unforgettable trip for both of us.

👄 본문 소리 내어 읽기

About 20 years ago, / I went on my honeymoon / with my husband. We didn't want to go to a typical resort. Instead, / we wanted to go somewhere special. So, / we decided to go to Italy, / which was full of history, art, and culture. However, / the trip didn't go / as smoothly as we had imagined. In Rome, we were pickpocketed / while walking on the street. We were so frustrated / and ended up having a big argument / that night. But afterwards, / we put our heads together / to figure out / how to get through this situation. At the same time, / we were amazed by the famous cultural landmarks, / like the Colosseum. It was breathtaking / to see them in person. We also enjoyed amazing local dishes, / which helped us forget about the bad experiences. Looking back now, / I can laugh about all those experiences. That honeymoon taught us / how to face challenges together / as a team. It was far from perfect, / but it was an unforgettable trip for both of us.

🗣 스피킹1_ 중요 패턴 익히기

decide to 동사원형 : ~하기로 결심하다

- I decided to stay home tonight. I think I need some time to recharge.

- I was shocked by my last check-up, so I decided to drink less.

- I decided not to start my own business because the economy is too bad.

- We decided not to buy that house. The price was way over our budget.

 **34강** 잊지 못할 여행

👄 **스피킹2_ 내 이야기해 봅시다**

Q Do you have any unforgettable trips?

A ▪ My unforgettable trip was to Jeju Island. The scenery was breathtaking, and I really enjoyed the local dishes.

▪ I will never forget the trip to Switzerland. The views were just like a painting and everything was so expensive.

▪ Seven years ago, I went to Sydney. It was an unforgettable trip because my child suddenly got sick, and we had to go to the emergency room.

34강 잊지 못할 여행

◎ **본문 [해석]**

약 20년 전, 나는 남편과 함께 신혼여행을 갔다. 우리는 흔한 휴양지로 가고 싶지 않았다. 대신, 특별한 곳으로 가고 싶었다. 그래서 우리는 역사와 예술, 문화로 가득한 이탈리아로 가기로 결정했다.

그러나 여행은 우리가 상상했던 것처럼 순탄하지 않았다. 로마에서 우리는 길을 걷다가 소매치기를 당했다. 우리는 매우 좌절했고, 그날 밤 큰 다툼을 벌이게 되었다. 하지만 이후, 우리는 머리를 맞대고 이 상황을 어떻게 헤쳐나갈지 고민했다.

동시에, 우리는 콜로세움과 같은 유명한 문화 유적지에 감탄했다. 실제로 그 장소들을 보니 숨이 멎을 만큼 놀라웠다. 우리는 또한 놀라운 현지 음식을 즐겼고, 그 덕분에 나쁜 경험들을 잊을 수 있었다.

돌아보면, 이제는 그 모든 경험들이 웃음이 난다. 그 신혼여행은 우리에게 한 팀으로서 문제에 대처하는 법을 가르쳐주었다. 완벽하진 않았지만, 우리 둘에게 잊을 수 없는 여행이었다.

34강 잊지 못할 여행

👄 **스피킹1_ 중요 패턴 익히기 [해석]**

decide to 동사원형 : ~하기로 결심하다

- 나는 오늘 밤 집에 있기로 결정했어요. 내 생각에 충전할 시간이 필요할 것 같아요.

- 최근 건강 검진 결과에 충격을 받았어요. 그래서 술을 줄이기로 결심했어요.

- 경기가 너무 안 좋아서 나는 창업하지 않기로 결심했어요.

- 우리는 그 집을 사지 않기로 결정했어요. 가격이 우리의 예산을 훨씬 초과했거든요.

👄 **스피킹2_ 내 이야기해 봅시다 [해석]**

질문 잊지 못할 여행이 있나요?

답
- 내가 잊지 못할 여행은 제주도였다. 경치는 숨이 멎을 만큼 아름다웠고, 현지 음식을 정말 즐겼다.

- 스위스 여행은 절대 잊을 수 없다. 풍경은 마치 그림 같았고, 모든 것이 정말 비쌌다.

- 7년 전 나는 시드니에 갔다. 그 여행은 잊을 수 없는데, 갑자기 아이가 아파서 응급실에 가야 했기 때문이다.

 **35강** 어린 시절 꿈

◉ 본문 **눈으로 이해하기**

Alice : Jinsu, what did you want to be when you were a child?

Jinsu : I wanted to be a scientist. I was curious about how things work. What about you?

Alice : That's so cool. In my case, I wanted to be a writer. I loved books that gave deep insights into people and life.

Jinsu : Oh, I see. What writer did you like the most?

Alice : I liked Charles Dickens, who wrote "Great Expectations".

Jinsu : I've heard of the book, but I haven't read it. Do you still want to be a writer?

Alice : Not really. Now, I just write as a hobby. What about you? Do you have someone you admire?

Jinsu : Yes, I admire King Sejong. He created Hangeul, and it helped so many people learn to read and write.

Alice : That's amazing! I've heard of him because I'm learning Korean. Hangeul is such a creative and brilliant system.

Jinsu : That's great to hear! How about you? Who do you admire?

Alice : I admire Mother Teresa. Her kindness and dedication to others are so inspiring.

Jinsu : She was truly incredible. I think both King Sejong and Mother Teresa made a big difference in the world.

Alice :   You can say that again!

35강 어린 시절 꿈

👄 **본문 소리 내어 읽기**

Alice : Jinsu, / what did you want to be / when you were a child?

Jinsu : I wanted to be a scientist. I was curious about / how things work. What about you?

Alice : That's so cool. In my case, / I wanted to be a writer. I loved books / that gave deep insights / into people and life.

Jinsu : Oh, I see. What writer did you like the most?

Alice : I liked Charles Dickens, / who wrote "Great Expectations".

Jinsu : I've heard of the book, / but I haven't read it. Do you still want to be a writer?

Alice : Not really. Now, / I just write / as a hobby. What about you? Do you have someone / you admire?

Jinsu : Yes, I admire King Sejong. He created Hangeul, / and it helped so many people / learn to read and write.

Alice : That's amazing! I've heard of him / because I'm learning Korean. Hangeul is such a creative and brilliant system.

Jinsu : That's great to hear! How about you? Who do you admire?

Alice : I admire Mother Teresa. Her kindness and dedication to others / are so inspiring.

Jinsu : She was truly incredible. I think / both King Sejong and Mother Teresa / made a big difference / in the world.

Alice : You can say that again!

35강 어린 시절 꿈

I've heard of 명사/대명사/동명사 : ~에 대해 들어본 적이 있다

- I've heard of that movie, but I haven't seen it yet.

- I've heard of her. She's a well-known author in Korea, right?

- I've heard of this brand. People say their products are high-quality.

- I've heard of that company. It has a great reputation.

 **35강** 어린 시절 꿈

👄 **스피킹2_ 내 이야기해 봅시다**

Q What did you want to be when you were a child?

A ■ I wanted to be an athlete because I enjoyed playing sports and was good at them.

■ I wanted to be a doctor because I wanted to help sick people in need, like Schweitzer.

■ I wanted to be a celebrity because I liked being in front of people and enjoyed getting attention.

■ I wanted to be a pilot because I dreamed of flying and seeing the world. And I made that dream come true.

어린 시절 꿈

👁 본문 [해석]

Alice : 진수, 어렸을 때 뭐가 되고 싶었어?

Jinsu : 과학자가 되고 싶었어. 나는 사물이 어떻게 작동하는지 궁금했거든. 너는?

Alice : 정말 멋지다! 나는 작가가 되고 싶었어. 사람들과 삶에 대한 깊은 통찰을 주는 책들을 좋아했거든.

Jinsu : 아, 그렇구나. 어떤 작가를 가장 좋아했어?

Alice : 나는 '위대한 유산'을 쓴 찰스 디킨스를 좋아했어.

Jinsu : 그 책에 대해 들어본 적은 있지만 읽어보진 않았어. 여전히 작가가 되고 싶어?

Alice : 꼭 그렇진 않아. 이제는 그냥 취미로 글을 써. 너는 어때? 존경하는 사람이 있어?

Jinsu : 응, 나는 세종대왕을 존경해. 그는 한글을 창제해서 많은 사람들이 읽고 쓰는 법을 배우는 데 도움을 줬거든.

Alice : 대단하다! 나도 그분에 대해 들어본 적 있어. 한국어를 배우고 있거든. 한글은 정말 창의적이고 훌륭한 체계야.

Jinsu : 그 말을 들으니 좋다! 너는 어때? 존경하는 사람이 있어?

Alice : 나는 마더 테레사를 존경해. 그녀의 친절과 타인에 대한 헌신이 정말 감동적이야.

Jinsu : 정말 대단한 분이지. 세종대왕과 마더 테레사는 둘 다 세상을 크게 바꾼 분들이라고 생각해.

Alice : 동감이야!

👄 스피킹1_ 중요 패턴 익히기 [해석]

I've heard of 명사/대명사/동명사 : ~에 대해 들어본 적이 있다

- 나는 그 영화에 대해 들어본 적은 있지만, 아직 보지는 않았어.

- 나는 그녀에 대해 들어본 적 있어. 그녀는 한국에서 유명한 작가 맞지?

- 나는 이 브랜드에 대해 들어본 적 있어. 사람들은 이 브랜드 제품이 품질이 좋다고 말해.

- 나는 그 회사에 대해 들어본 적 있어. 그 회사는 평판이 정말 좋아.

👄 스피킹2_ 내 이야기해 봅시다 [해석]

질문 어렸을 때가 뭐가 되고 싶었나요?

답
- 나는 운동을 즐겼고 잘했기 때문에 운동선수가 되고 싶었어요.

- 나는 도움이 필요한 아픈 사람들을 돕고 싶어서, 슈바이처처럼 의사가 되고 싶었어요.

- 나는 사람들 앞에 서는 것을 좋아했고 주목받는 것을 즐겼기 때문에 연예인이 되고 싶었어요.

- 나는 하늘을 날며 세상을 보는 걸 꿈꿔서 파일럿이 되고 싶었어요. 그리고 그 꿈을 이루었어요.

 **36강**  한국의 분리수거 시스템

👁 본문 눈으로 이해하기

<Korea's Recycling System>

Korea has a very organized recycling system. People must separate their trash into different categories, such as plastic, paper, glass, metal, and food waste. Each category has its own bin or bag. For example, food waste goes into a special food waste bin. This waste is later used to make animal feed or fertilizer.

Recyclable items like plastic and glass bottles must be cleaned before recycling. Also, people must remove labels or caps from bottles. Depending on the area, there are specific days to put out different types of trash for collection.

Recycling is important in Korea because it helps reduce waste and protect the environment. The government encourages people to recycle and provides clear guidelines. Fines can be given to those who do not follow the rules. Korea is currently one of the world's leading examples of effective recycling and waste separation.

👄 **본문 소리 내어 읽기**

<Korea's Recycling System>

Korea has a very organized recycling system. People must separate their trash / into different categories, / such as plastic, paper, glass, metal, and food waste. Each category has its own bin or bag. For example, / food waste goes / into a special food waste bin. This waste is later used / to make animal feed or fertilizer.

Recyclable items / like plastic and glass bottles / must be cleaned / before recycling. Also, / people must remove labels or caps / from bottles. Depending on the area, / there are specific days / to put out different types of trash / for collection.

Recycling is important in Korea / because it helps reduce waste / and protect the environment. The government encourages people to recycle / and provides clear guidelines. Fines can be given / to those who do not follow the rules. Korea is currently / one of the world's leading examples / of effective recycling and waste separation.

한국의 분리수거 시스템

🗣 **스피킹1_ 중요 패턴 익히기**

encourage A to 동사원형 : ~하기를 권장하다, 격려하다

- My friend encouraged me to apply for the job, and I finally got it.

- My parents trusted me completely, and encouraged me to pursue my dream.

- We should encourage our children to be independent. Then, they can live their lives on their own.

 **36강** 한국의 분리수거 시스템

👄 **스피킹2_ 내 이야기해 봅시다**

Q Do you recycle? If so, how often do you recycle trash?

A
- Of course. In my neighborhood, we can put out recyclable trash every Thursday. And it's my responsibility in my family.

- I do. In my apartment, we put out recyclable trash twice a week, on Tuesdays and Fridays.

- I'm living abroad now, and there's no separate recycling system in my area. Everything goes into one bin.

한국의 분리수거 시스템

◎ 본문 [해석]

한국은 매우 체계적인 재활용 시스템을 가지고 있다. 사람들은 쓰레기를 플라스틱, 종이, 유리, 금속, 음식물 쓰레기 등으로 분리해야 한다. 각 분류에는 전용 쓰레기통이나 봉투가 있다. 예를 들어, 음식물 쓰레기는 전용 음식물 쓰레기통에 버려야 한다. 이 쓰레기는 나중에 동물 사료나 비료를 만드는 데 사용된다.

플라스틱이나 유리 병 같은 재활용 가능한 물품은 재활용하기 전에 깨끗이 씻어야 한다. 또한, 병의 라벨이나 뚜껑을 제거해야 한다. 지역에 따라 수거를 위해 서로 다른 종류의 쓰레기를 내놓는 정해진 요일이 있다.

한국에서 재활용은 중요하다. 왜냐하면 이것이 쓰레기를 줄이고 환경을 보호하는 데 도움이 되기 때문이다. 정부는 사람들이 재활용을 하도록 권장하며 명확한 지침을 제공한다. 규칙을 따르지 않는 사람들에게는 벌금이 부과될 수 있다. 한국은 효과적인 재활용 및 분리수거에 대해 현재 세계에서 모범 사례 중 하나이다.

한국의 분리수거 시스템

🗣 스피킹1_ 중요 패턴 익히기 [해석]

encourage A to 동사원형 : ~하기를 권장하다, 격려하다

- 내 친구는 내가 그 일자리에 지원하도록 격려했고, 결국 나는 그 일을 얻게 되었다.

- 우리 부모님은 나를 전적으로 믿으셨고, 내 꿈을 추구하도록 격려해 주셨다.

- 우리는 아이들이 독립적이 되도록 격려해야 한다. 그러면 그들은 스스로 자신의 삶을 살아갈 수 있을 것이다.

🗣 스피킹2_ 내 이야기해 봅시다 [해석]

질문 분리수거 하시나요? 그렇다면, 얼마나 자주 분리수거 하나요?

답
- 물론이죠. 내가 사는 동네에서는 매주 목요일에 재활용 쓰레기를 내놓을 수 있습니다. 그리고 이것은 우리 가족에서 제 책임입니다.

- 네, 합니다. 제가 사는 아파트에서는 일주일에 두 번, 화요일과 금요일에 재활용 쓰레기를 내놓습니다.

- 저는 지금 해외에 살고 있는데, 제가 사는 지역에는 분리수거 시스템이 따로 없습니다. 모든 쓰레기를 한 통에 모아서 버립니다.

37강 잔소리

Mom : Daniel, did you hear it's going to rain today?

Daniel : I know, Mom.

Mom : Don't forget your umbrella, okay?

Daniel : Alright, alright...

Mom : And make sure to close the windows before you leave. Otherwise, rain might get in and make a mess.

Daniel : Alright, I'll do it.

Mom : Did you brush your hair? It looks messy.

Daniel : Mom, seriously?

Mom : I'm just saying, you don't want to look like you just rolled out of bed.

Daniel : Mom, can you stop? I've got this.

Mom : I'm only trying to help you.

Daniel : I know, but I can take care of myself. Please, no more nagging.

Mom : Fine, have it your way.

(A little later)

Daniel : Oh no! I forgot my math homework! Mom, do you know where it is?

Mom : Didn't you just say you didn't need my help?

Daniel : Mom, this is serious! Please help me!

37강 잔소리

👄 본문 소리 내어 읽기

Mom : Daniel, / did you hear / it's going to rain today?

Daniel : I know, Mom.

Mom : Don't forget your umbrella, okay?

Daniel : Alright, alright...

Mom : And make sure to close the windows / before you leave. Otherwise, / rain might get in / and make a mess.

Daniel : Alright, I'll do it.

Mom : Did you brush your hair? It looks messy.

Daniel : Mom, seriously?

Mom : I'm just saying, / you don't want to look like / you just rolled out of bed.

Daniel : Mom, can you stop? I've got this.

Mom : I'm only trying to help you.

Daniel : I know, / but I can take care of myself. Please, no more nagging.

Mom : Fine, have it your way.

(A little later)

Daniel : Oh no! I forgot my math homework! Mom, do you know where it is?

Mom : Didn't you just say / you didn't need my help?

Daniel : Mom, this is serious! Please help me!

🗣 스피킹1_ 중요 패턴 익히기

Did you hear 주어 + 동사 : (주어)가 (동사)하는 거 들었어?

- Did you hear what happened to Sarah? She got a promotion at work. I'm happy for her.

- Did you hear she's getting married? I had no idea she was seeing someone!

- Did you hear the news about our company? Our office is moving to a new location.

👄 **스피킹2_ 내 이야기해 봅시다**

Q **Do you often nag your kids? If so, what's it usually about?**

A
- Yes, I often nag my son about cleaning his room. It's really messy.

- All the time! It's usually about their phones, because they're always on them.

- I try not to, but sometimes I can't help it when they don't listen.

- Which parent doesn't? Nagging is part of everyday life.

잔소리

👁 본문 [해석]

Mom : 다니엘, 오늘 비 온다고 들었니?

Daniel : 응, 알아요, 엄마.

Mom : 우산 챙기는 거 잊지 마, 알겠지?

Daniel : 알았어요, 알았어...

Mom : 그리고 나가기 전에 창문 꼭 닫아. 안 그러면 비가 들어와서 엉망이 될지도 몰라.

Daniel : 알았어요, 할게요.

Mom : 머리 빗었니? 헝클어진 것 같아.

Daniel : 엄마, 제발요.

Mom : 그냥 말하는 거야. 막 침대에서 굴러나온 것처럼 보이고 싶진 않잖아.

Daniel : 엄마, 그만할래요? 제가 알아서 해요.

Mom : 난 그냥 널 도우려는 거야.

Daniel : 알아요. 하지만 제가 알아서 할 수 있어요. 제발, 잔소리는 그만해주세요.

Mom : 그래, 네가 원하는 대로 해.

(잠시 뒤)

Daniel : 아, 이런! 수학 숙제를 깜빡했어요! 엄마, 어디 있는지 아세요?

Mom : 방금 전에 내 도움이 필요 없다고 하지 않았니?

Daniel : 엄마, 지금 진지한 상황이에요! 도와주세요!

스피킹1_ 중요 패턴 익히기 [해석]

Did you hear 주어 + 동사 : (주어)가 (동사)하는 거 들었어?

- 사라에게 무슨 일이 있었는지 들었어? 그녀가 직장에서 승진했대. 정말 기쁘다.

- 그녀가 결혼한다는 얘기 들었어? ㅠㅠ그녀가 누구를 만나고 있었는지 전혀 몰랐어!

- 우리 회사에 대한 소식 들었어? 우리 사무실이 새로운 장소로 이전한대.

스피킹2_ 내 이야기해 봅시다 [해석]

질문 아이들에게 잔소리 자주 하시나요? 그렇다면 주로 뭐에 대한 건가요?

답
- 네, 저는 아들에게 방 청소하라고 자주 잔소리해요. 진짜 더럽거든요.

- 항상요! 주로 핸드폰에 대한 건데, 항상 핸드폰 보고 있거든요.

- 안 하려고 하는데요, 하지만 가끔씩 말 안 들을 땐, 저도 어쩔 수 없네요.

- 어느 부모가 안 할까요? 잔소리는 일상입니다.

38강 K-Food

👁 **본문 눈으로 이해하기**

K-Food is gaining popularity all over the world. Many people enjoy dishes like bulgogi, japchae, and bibimbap. These dishes are tasty, healthy, and full of rich flavors.

One reason K-Food is becoming more popular is Korean culture, like movies, dramas, and K-pop. Fans of K-culture see their favorite stars eating Korean food, like ramyeon, and this makes them want to try it too. Another reason is that Korean food uses many different ingredients and seasonings to make rich and unique flavors.

Eating Korean food is also a fun and exciting experience. For example, when you eat Korean barbecue like samgyeopsal, you can watch the meat cook on a charcoal grill right in front of you. You can wrap the meat in lettuce, which is called ssam, or make fried rice with the leftover sauce. All these things spark the curiosity of foreigners.

Have you tried K-Food yet? If not, you should give it a try. It might open up a whole new world for you!

38강 K-Food

👄 본문 소리 내어 읽기

K-Food is gaining popularity / all over the world. Many people enjoy dishes / like bulgogi, japchae, and bibimbap. These dishes are tasty, healthy, / and full of rich flavors. One reason K-Food is becoming more popular / is Korean culture, / like movies, dramas, and K-pop. Fans of K-culture / see their favorite stars eating Korean food, / like ramyeon, / and this makes them want to try it too. Another reason is that / Korean food uses many different ingredients and seasonings / to make rich and unique flavors.

Eating Korean food / is also a fun and exciting experience. For example, / when you eat Korean barbecue like samgyeopsal, / you can watch the meat cook / on a charcoal grill / right in front of you. You can wrap the meat in lettuce, / which is called ssam, / or make fried rice / with the leftover sauce. All these things spark / the curiosity of foreigners.

Have you tried K-Food yet? If not, / you should give it a try. It might open up / a whole new world for you!

K-Food

👄 스피킹1_ 중요 패턴 익히기

지각동사(see, watch, hear, listen to, feel) + A(목적어) + 동사원형/동사ing : A가 (동사)하는 것을 (보다, 지켜보다, 듣다, 유심히 듣다, 느끼다)

- I saw him cross the street.

  I saw him crossing the street.

- I heard her sing a song.

  I heard her singing a song.

- I felt something touch my shoulder, but when I turned around, there was no one.

- I felt something touching my shoulder, and it turned out to be a spider.

 **K-Food**

👄 **스피킹2_ 내 이야기해 봅시다**

Q **Have you ever tried Korean food?**
If not, is there any Korean food you want to try?

A ▪ Yes, I have and I love it! My favorite is gimbap.

▪ Of course! I've been to a Korean restaurant several

times. I really like japchae. I could eat it every day.

▪ Not yet, but I really want to try Korean barbeque. It

looks delicious!

K-Food

K-Food는 전 세계적으로 인기를 얻고 있습니다. 많은 사람들이 불고기, 잡채, 비빔밥과 같은 요리를 즐깁니다. 이러한 요리들은 맛있고 건강하며, 풍부한 맛이 가득합니다.

K-Food가 점점 더 인기를 얻고 있는 한 가지 이유는 영화, 드라마, K-pop과 같은 한국 문화 때문입니다. K-컬처 팬들은 자신이 좋아하는 스타들이 라면과 같은 한국 음식을 먹는 것을 보고, 이를 먹어보고 싶어 합니다. 또 다른 이유는 한국 음식이 다양한 재료와 양념을 사용해 독특하고 깊은 맛을 만들어내기 때문입니다.

한국 음식을 먹는 것 자체도 재미있고 신나는 경험입니다. 예를 들어, 삼겹살 같은 한국식 바비큐를 먹을 때, 바로 앞에서 숯불 위에서 고기가 익는 모습을 볼 수 있습니다. 고기를 상추에 싸서 먹을 수도 있고, 남은 소스로 볶음밥을 만들어 먹을 수도 있습니다. 이러한 모든 것들이 외국인의 호기심을 자극합니다.

K-Food를 먹어본 적 있나요? 아직 먹어보지 않았다면 꼭 한 번 시도해 보세요. 아마도 당신에게 새로운 세상을 열어줄지도 모릅니다.

K-Food

지각동사(see, watch, hear, listen to, feel) + A(목적어) + 동사원형/동사ing : A가 (동사)하는 것을 (보다, 지켜보다, 듣다, 유심히 듣다, 느끼다)

■ 나는 그가 길을 건너는 것을 보았다.

(cross) 길을 건너는 동작 전체를 보았다.

(crossing) 길을 건너는 중인 모습을 보았다.

■ 나는 그녀가 노래를 부르는 것을 들었다.

(sing) 노래를 처음부터 끝까지 부르는 전체 과정을 들었다.

(singing) 노래를 부르고 있는 중인 순간을 들었다.

■ 나는 어깨를 무언가가 건드리는 것을 느꼈지만, 돌아보니 아무도 없었다.

■ 나는 어깨를 무언가가 건드리고 있는 것을 느꼈고, 알고 보니 그것은 거미였다.

38강 K-Food

🗣 **스피킹2_ 내 이야기해 봅시다 [해석]**

질문
혹시 한국 음식 먹어본 적 있나요?
없다면, 먹어보고 싶은 한국 음식이 있나요?

답
- 네, 먹어본 적 있고 정말 좋아해요! 제가 가장 좋아하는 것은 김밥이에요.

- 물론이죠! 저는 한국 식당에 여러 번 가봤어요. 잡채를 정말 좋아해요. 매일 먹을 수도 있을 것 같아요.

- 아직 먹어보진 않았지만, 한국 바비큐를 정말 먹어보고 싶어요. 정말 맛있어 보여요!

MEMO

39강 런던에 가본 적 있나요?

👁 본문 눈으로 이해하기

Alice : Hey, Jinsu, have you ever been to London?

Jinsu : Yeah, I went there when I was a university student on a backpacking trip.

Alice : That's amazing! I've never been to London, but I love British literature. I really want to visit someday.

Jinsu : You should! There's so much to see there.

Alice : Did you go to the British Museum?

Jinsu : Of course! It's huge. Even if you spend the whole day there, you can't see everything. And also, the admission was free, so I didn't have to worry about the cost.

Alice : That sounds incredible! What was the weather like?

Jinsu : Honestly, it wasn't great. It was often cloudy and rainy.

Alice : Just like I've heard. What about the food?

Jinsu : The food wasn't very good either, but there were plenty of other options, like pasta and curry.

Alice : That's good to know! How were the people there?

Jinsu : Most people were kind and polite. That made the trip much better.

Alice : I hope I can go there soon. I can't wait!

👄 본문 소리 내어 읽기

Alice : Hey, Jinsu, / have you ever been to London?

Jinsu : Yeah, I went there / when I was a university student / on a backpacking trip.

Alice : That's amazing! I've never been to London, / but I love British literature. I really want to visit someday.

Jinsu : You should! There's so much / to see there.

Alice : Did you go to the British Museum?

Jinsu : Of course! It's huge. Even if you spend the whole day there, / you can't see everything. And also, / the admission was free, / so I didn't have to worry about the cost.

Alice : That sounds incredible! What was the weather like?

Jinsu : Honestly, / it wasn't great. It was often cloudy and rainy.

Alice : Just like I've heard. What about the food?

Jinsu : The food wasn't very good either, / but there were plenty of other options, / like pasta and curry.

Alice : That's good to know! How were the people there?

Jinsu : Most people were kind and polite. That made the trip much better.

Alice : I hope / I can go there soon. I can't wait!

스피킹1_ 중요 패턴 익히기

even if 주어 + 동사 : (주어)가 (동사)라 할지라도, ~라 해도

- Even if I'm tired, I always walk my dog in the evening.

- Even if it rains tomorrow, the event will still take place.

- Even if you fail, it's okay. You can try again.

- Even if you don't have experience, you can still apply.

👄 **스피킹2_ 내 이야기해 봅시다**

Q **Have you ever been to London?**

A ■ Yes, I visited London during my trip to Europe. It was an impressive city.

■ Yes, I have, but it wasn't my favorite place. The weather was especially bad.

■ Not yet, but I'd like to go there someday. I want to watch a musical in the West End.

■ No, I haven't, but it's on my bucket list. I heard that it's a beautiful city.

◎ 본문 [해석]

Alice : 진수, 혹시 런던 가본 적 있어?

Jinsu : 응, 대학생 때 배낭여행으로 갔었어.

Alice : 정말 놀랍다! 나는 런던에 가본 적 없지만, 영국 문학을 정말 좋아해. 언젠가 꼭 가보고 싶어.

Jinsu : 꼭 가봐! 거기에 볼 게 정말 많아.

Alice : 대영박물관에 갔었어?

Jinsu : 당연하지! 엄청 커. 하루 종일 있어도 다 볼 수 없을 정도야. 그리고 입장료도 무료라서 비용 걱정을 안 해도 됐어.

Alice : 정말 놀랍다! 날씨는 어땠어?

Jinsu : 솔직히 별로였어. 자주 흐리고 비가 왔어.

Alice : 듣던 대로네. 음식은 어땠어?

Jinsu : 음식도 별로였어. 하지만 파스타나 커리 같은 다른 선택지가 많았어.

Alice : 그거 알아두면 좋네! 사람들은 어땠어?

Jinsu : 대부분 친절하고 예의 바른 사람들이었어. 덕분에 여행이 훨씬 더 좋았어.

Alice : 나도 빨리 가보고 싶다. 정말 기대돼!

런던에 가본 적 있나요?

👄 스피킹1_ 중요 패턴 익히기 [해석]

even if 주어 + 동사 : (주어)가 (동사)라 할지라도, ~라 해도

- 나는 피곤하더라도, 항상 저녁에 개를 산책시킨다.

- 내일 비가 오더라도, 그 행사는 열릴 것이다.

- 실패하더라도 괜찮아. 다시 시도하면 돼.

- 경험이 없더라도, 여전히 지원할 수 있다.

👄 스피킹2_ 내 이야기해 봅시다 [해석]

질문 혹시 런던에 가 본 적 있나요?

답
- 네, 유럽 여행 중에 런던을 방문했어요. 인상적인 도시였어요.

- 네, 가본 적 있지만 제 마음에 드는 곳은 아니었어요. 특히 날씨가 별로였어요.

- 아직은 아니지만, 언젠가 가보고 싶어요. 웨스트엔드에서 뮤지컬을 보고 싶어요.

- 아니요, 가 본 적은 없지만 제 버킷리스트에 있어요. 아름다운 도시라고 들었어요.

40강 인간관계

◉ **본문 눈으로 이해하기**

<How to Have Good Relationships with Others>

A good relationship starts with respect and understanding. When you listen well, the other person feels valued. Instead of just talking about yourself, ask questions and show interest in their thoughts.

Showing kindness and care is also important. Small things, like remembering someone's birthday or asking if they are okay, can make a big difference. When people feel that you truly care, they will also treat you well.

However, not all relationships are easy. Sometimes, you meet people who are difficult to get along with. In these cases, try not to let your emotions control you. Stay calm and don't take everything personally.

If a relationship makes you too stressed, it is okay to take some distance. Your mental health is important, and sometimes, stepping away is the best choice.

In short, be kind to others, but also take care of yourself. This way, you can have good relationships and feel happy too.

40강 인간관계

👄 **본문 소리 내어 읽기**

<How to Have Good Relationships with Others>

A good relationship starts **/** with respect and understanding. When you listen well, **/** the other person feels valued. Instead of just talking about yourself, **/** ask questions **/** and show interest **/** in their thoughts.

Showing kindness and care **/** is also important. Small things, **/** like remembering someone's birthday **/** or asking if they are okay, **/** can make a big difference. When people feel that you truly care, **/** they will also treat you well.

However, **/** not all relationships are easy. Sometimes, **/** you meet people **/** who are difficult **/** to get along with. In these cases, **/** try not to let your emotions control you. Stay calm **/** and don't take everything personally.

If a relationship makes you too stressed, **/** it is okay **/** to take some distance. Your mental health is important, **/** and sometimes, **/** stepping away is the best choice.

In short, **/** be kind to others, **/** but also take care of yourself. This way, **/** you can have good relationships **/** and feel happy too.

40강 인간관계

👄 **스피킹1_ 중요 패턴 익히기**

ask if 주어 + 동사 : (주어)가 (동사) 인지 물어보다

- I'll ask if he is available tomorrow. If not, we can find another time.

- Can you ask if she is coming this Saturday? I hope so. I haven't seen her in a while.

- Ask if he wants something to drink. We have coffee, green tea, and orange juice.

 **40강** 인간관계

Q How do you maintain a good relationship with others?

A
- I try to keep in touch with my friends, so we don't grow apart.

- I text my friends to check in, and sometimes make plans to meet up.

- I'm not the type to reach out first, but I respond warmly when someone contacts me.

- I'm not a very social person, but I avoid talking behind people's backs.

👁 본문 [해석]

<좋은 인간관계를 유지하는 방법>

좋은 관계는 존중과 이해에서 시작된다. 네가 잘 들어주면, 상대방은 존중받는다고 느낀다. 자기 이야기만 하는 대신, 질문을 하고 상대방의 생각에 관심을 보이는 것이 중요하다.

친절과 배려를 보이는 것도 중요하다. 생일을 기억하거나 상대방의 안부를 묻는 작은 행동이 큰 차이를 만들 수 있다. 사람들이 네가 진심으로 관심을 가진다고 느끼면, 그들도 너를 잘 대해 줄 것이다.

하지만, 모든 관계가 쉬운 것은 아니다. 때때로 잘 맞지 않는 사람을 만나게 될 수도 있다. 그런 경우에는 감정에 휘둘리지 않도록 노력해야 한다. 차분함을 유지하고, 모든 말을 개인적으로 받아들이지 않는 것이 좋다.

어떤 관계가 너에게 너무 큰 스트레스를 준다면, 거리를 두어도 괜찮다. 너의 정신 건강이 중요하며, 때로는 관계에서 한 발 물러서는 것이 최선의 선택일 수도 있다.

요컨대, 다른 사람들에게 친절하게 대하되, 너 자신도 소중히 여겨야 한다. 이렇게 하면 좋은 관계를 유지하면서도 행복할 수 있다.

40강 인간관계

👄 스피킹1_ 중요 패턴 익히기 [해석]

ask if 주어 + 동사 : (주어)가 (동사) 인지 물어보다

- 그가 내일 시간 되는지 물어볼게. 안 되면, 다른 시간을 찾으면 돼.

- 그녀가 이번 토요일에 오는지 물어봐 줄래? 그랬으면 좋겠어. 한동안 그녀를 못 봤거든.

- 그가 마실 거 원하는지 물어봐. 커피, 녹차, 오렌지 주스가 있어.

👄 스피킹2_ 내 이야기해 봅시다 [해석]

질문 다른 사람들과 어떻게 좋은 관계를 유지하시나요?

답
- 나는 친구들과 연락을 유지하려고 노력합니다. 그래서 우리가 멀어지지 않도록요.

- 나는 친구들에게 안부를 묻는 문자를 보내고, 가끔 만나자는 약속을 잡습니다.

- 나는 먼저 연락하는 스타일은 아니지만, 누군가 연락을 하면 반갑게 응대합니다.

- 나는 사교적인 편은 아니지만, 뒷담화는 피하려고 합니다.

제나쌤의
영어리스닝
길잡이

죽어라 안들리던 영어가 드디어 들리기 시작한다!

토종 한국인 영어강사 본인과 지난 15년간
수많은 영어학습자들의 영어 귀를 트여준 검증된 학습법

#이런 분들께 이 책과 온라인강의를 추천드립니다

- ✦ 영어공부 나름 십수년 했는데 실력이 제자리같은 분
- ✦ 특히 눈으로는 대충 알겠는데, 막상 귀로 들으면 안들리는 분
- ✦ 리스닝이지만 리딩과 스피킹 실력도 동시에 함께 늘리고 싶은 분
- ✦ 나의 삶과 내가 사는 한국에 대해 영어로 어떻게 표현하는지 배우고 싶은 분

#학생들의 강의평

여지껏 영어공부는 듣기만 하고 눈으로만 했던 공부였는데, 내 입으로 말하고 녹음하니 너무 재밌었습니다. 외국인 친구에게 들려줬더니 너무 잘한다고 칭찬 받았어요. - 에*더님

소리내어 읽기가 진짜 많은 도움이 되어서 요즘 미드볼 때 소리가 블럭화되어 뇌를 밟고 지나가는 느낌으로 들려요. - 명*은 님

제나쌤 강의를 통해 습득된 영어표현이 현지에서 들리고, 배운 패턴문장을 적용하여 스피킹으로 출력하는 제 모습에 깜짝 놀랐습니다. - Five *님

직접 읽어보니 자신감도 늘고, 반복하면 할 수록 잘 읽혀지고 속도도 느는게 신기했어요. 공부하고 들으니 더 잘들렸구요. - 민*님

소리내어 읽으면 영어가 들린다

제나쌤의
영어리스닝
길잡이

나의 삶, 한국,
해외여행 편

3권

유튜브 채널 [길잡이영어]
[봄봄클래스] 강의교재

제나(김수연) 지음

전)EBS강사 제나쌤이 알려주는
효과만점 영어귀뚫기 7단계 학습법

 영어 학습 콘텐츠
유튜브 채널 [길잡이영어]

 제나쌤 온라인 강의
[봄봄클래스]

길잡이★북스

제나쌤의
영어리스닝
길잡이

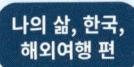

나의 삶, 한국,
해외여행 편

유튜브 채널 [길잡이영어]
[봄봄클래스] 강외교재

세나(김주연) 지음

길잡이★북스

CONTENTS

👁 **본문 눈으로 이해하기**

Jinsu : Hey Alice, did you eat?

Alice : Oh, not yet. Are you asking me to have lunch with you?

Jinsu : Oh! No, I just meant to say hi. In Korea, we ask "Did you eat?" as a greeting.

Alice : Oh, really? That's interesting! In America, we usually say, "How are you?" instead.

Jinsu : I see! I'll try to remember that when talking to Americans.

Alice : Yeah! But I like your way too. It feels warm and friendly.

Jinsu : Thanks!

Alice : By the way, Jinsu, your English is really good! I noticed it again.

Jinsu : Oh no, not really. I still make a lot of mistakes.

Alice : But you ARE good! Why do you say that?

Jinsu : Well, in Korea, we try to be humble. It's polite to say, "No, I'm not good."

Alice : Oh, I see! But in America, we just say "Thank you!" when we get a compliment.

Jinsu : Oh, really? That's much easier!

Alice : Right! Next time, just say "Thank you!"

Jinsu : Alright, I'll try! Thank you!

Alice : See? That was perfect!

문화차이

🗣 본문 소리 내어 읽기

Jinsu : Hey Alice, did you eat?

Alice : Oh, not yet. Are you asking me to have lunch with you?

Jinsu : Oh! No, I just meant to say hi. In Korea, / we ask "Did you eat?" / as a greeting.

Alice : Oh, really? That's interesting! In America, / we usually say, "How are you?" instead.

Jinsu : I see! I'll try to remember that / when talking to Americans.

Alice : Yeah! But I like your way too. It feels warm and friendly.

Jinsu : Thanks!

Alice : By the way, Jinsu, your English is really good! I noticed it again.

Jinsu : Oh no, not really. I still make a lot of mistakes.

Alice : But you ARE good! Why do you say that?

Jinsu : Well, in Korea, / we try to be humble. It's polite to say, / "No, I'm not good."

Alice : Oh, I see! But in America, / we just say "Thank you!" / when we get a compliment.

Jinsu : Oh, really? That's much easier!

Alice : Right! Next time, / just say "Thank you!"

Jinsu : Alright, I'll try! Thank you!

Alice : See? That was perfect!

문화차이

💋 **스피킹1_ 중요 패턴 익히기**

I meant to 동사원형 : ~할 의도였어, ~하려고 했어

- I meant to wake up early, but I overslept. I barely made it on time.

- I meant to tell you about it. But I didn't get the chance.

- I didn't mean to hurt you. But if I did, I'm really sorry.

- I didn't mean to say that. I wasn't thinking. I apologize.

👄 **스피킹2_ 내 이야기해 봅시다**

Q **Have you ever experienced culture shock in Korea?**

A
- I was surprised that people bow so often. At first, it was unfamiliar, but now I like it because it's polite.

- I didn't expect that asking someone's age was so common. In my country, it's a bit personal.

- I was amazed by how fast everything is, from food delivery to internet speed.

◎ 본문 [해석]

Jinsu : 앨리스! 밥 먹었어?

Alice : 아직 안 먹었어. 나랑 점심 먹자고 묻는 거야?

Jinsu : 아! 아니야, 난 그냥 인사하려고 했어. 한국에서는 "밥 먹었어?"라고 인사해.

Alice : 아, 정말? 흥미롭다! 미국에서는 보통 "잘 지내?"라고 말해.

Jinsu : 그렇구나! 미국인과 이야기할 때 기억하도록 할게.

Alice : 응! 하지만 너희 방식도 좋은 것 같아. 따뜻하고 친근한 느낌이야.

Jinsu : 고마워.

Alice : 그런데 진수야, 너 영어 정말 잘한다! 다시 한 번 느꼈어.

Jinsu : 아냐, 전혀. 난 아직도 실수를 많이 해.

Alice : 하지만 정말 잘하는데! 왜 그렇게 말해?

Jinsu : 음, 한국에서는 겸손해야 해. 그래서 "아니, 나 못해."라고 말하는 게 예의야.

Alice : 아, 그렇구나! 하지만 미국에서는 칭찬을 받으면 그냥 "고마워!"라고 해.

Jinsu : 아, 그래? 그게 훨씬 쉽다!

Alice : 맞아! 다음번엔 그냥 "고마워!"라고 말해 봐!

Jinsu : 알겠어, 해 볼게! 고마워!

Alice : 봐! 완벽했어!

문화차이

👄 **스피킹1_ 중요 패턴 익히기 [해석]**

I meant to 동사원형 : ~할 의도였어, ~하려고 했어

- 일찍 일어나려고 했는데 늦잠을 잤어. 간신히 시간 맞춰 도착했어.

- 너한테 그 얘기 하려고 했는데, 기회가 없었어.

- 널 상처 주려던 게 아니었어. 하지만 그랬다면, 정말 미안해.

- 그렇게 말하려던 게 아니었어. 내가 생각 없이 말했어. 미안해.

👄 **스피킹2_ 내 이야기해 봅시다 [해석]**

질문 혹시 한국에서 문화 충격을 경험한 적이 있나요?

답 ■ 사람들이 그렇게 자주 인사할 때 고개를 숙이는 게 놀라웠어요.

처음엔 익숙하지 않았는데, 이제는 예의 바른 것 같아 좋아요.

■ 누군가의 나이를 묻는 것이 이렇게 흔할 줄은 예상하지 못했어요. 제 나라에서는 조금 개인적인 질문이에요.

■ 음식 배달부터 인터넷 속도까지, 모든 것이 너무 빠른 게 놀라웠어요.

 **42강**  한국에 살면 좋은 점

◎ **본문 눈으로 이해하기**

I have lived in Korea for seven years. I love many things about life here. One of the best things is the public transportation. The subway and buses are clean, safe, and always on time. It's easy to get around the city without a car.

Korea is also very safe. I enjoy taking walks in the park near my place, and even at night, there are many people around, so I don't feel scared.

Another thing I love is Korean food and the delivery culture. Korean food has a lot of variety, and there are many tasty and healthy options. Also, food delivery is super fast, and I can order almost anything.

Finally, the people in Korea are one of the best parts of living here. Koreans are kind and warm, and they are always willing to help. Even though I'm a foreigner, I always feel welcome.

Living in Korea has been a great experience, and I hope to stay here for as long as possible.

👄 **본문 소리 내어 읽기**

I have lived in Korea **/** for seven years. I love many things **/** about life here. One of the best things **/** is the public transportation. The subway and buses are clean, safe, **/** and always on time. It's easy to get around the city **/** without a car.

Korea is also very safe. I enjoy taking walks **/** in the park **/** near my place, **/** and even at night, **/** there are many people around, **/** so I don't feel scared.

Another thing I love **/** is Korean food **/** and the delivery culture. Korean food has a lot of variety, **/** and there are many tasty and healthy options. Also, **/** food delivery is super fast, **/** and I can order almost anything.

Finally, **/** the people in Korea **/** are one of the best parts **/** of living here. Koreans are kind and warm, **/** and they are always willing to help. Even though I'm a foreigner, **/** I always feel welcome.

Living in Korea has been a great experience, **/** and I hope to stay here **/** for as long as possible.

한국에 살면 좋은 점

👄 스피킹1_ 중요 패턴 익히기

There is + 단수명사 : ~가 있다
There are + 복수명사 : ~들이 있다

- There is a restroom over there, but it's out of order.

- There is a problem with my phone. The battery drains too fast.

- There are a few cars on the road, but overall, the traffic is light.

- There are no classes tomorrow, so I'm going to sleep in and then hang out with my friends.

 **42강** **한국에 살면 좋은 점**

👄 **스피킹2_ 내 이야기해 봅시다**

Q **How do you like living in Korea?**

A
- It's great! Living here is really safe and convenient.

- I enjoy living in Korea. There are so many good things about it, but sometimes, I miss home and my family.

- It's a bit challenging. I'm still getting used to the culture and language.

한국에 살면 좋은 점

👁 본문 [해석]

나는 한국에서 7년 동안 살았다. 나는 이곳에서의 삶에서 많은 것을 좋아한다. 그중 하나는 대중교통이다. 지하철과 버스는 깨끗하고, 안전하며, 항상 제시간에 온다. 차 없이도 도시를 돌아다니기 쉽다.

한국은 또한 매우 안전한 곳이다. 나는 집 근처 공원에서 산책하는 것을 즐기는데, 밤에도 사람들이 많아서 무섭지 않다.

또 내가 좋아하는 것은 한국 음식과 배달 문화이다. 한국 음식은 종류가 다양하고, 맛있고 건강한 선택지가 많다. 또한, 음식 배달이 매우 빠르고, 거의 모든 음식을 주문할 수 있다.

마지막으로, 한국에서 사는 것의 가장 좋은 점 중 하나는 사람들이다. 한국 사람들은 친절하고 따뜻하며, 항상 도와주려고 한다. 나는 외국인이지만, 항상 환영받는 느낌을 받는다.

한국에서 사는 것은 정말 좋은 경험이었고, 나는 가능하면 오래 머물고 싶다.

한국에 살면 좋은 점

👄 **스피킹1_ 중요 패턴 익히기 [해석]**

There is + 단수명사 : ~가 있다
There are + 복수명사 : ~들이 있다

- 저쪽에 화장실이 있지만, 고장 났어요.

- 내 폰에 문제가 있어. 배터리가 너무 빨리 닳아.

- 도로에 차가 몇 대 있지만, 대체로 교통이 원활해.

- 내일 수업이 없어서 늦잠 자고, 그다음에 친구들이랑 놀 거야.

👄 **스피킹2_ 내 이야기해 봅시다 [해석]**

질문 한국에 사는 것 어떠세요?

답
- 정말 좋아요! 여기에서 사는 것은 정말 안전하고 편리해요.

- 한국에서 사는 게 즐거워요. 좋은 점이 정말 많아요. 하지만 가끔은 집과 가족이 그리워요.

- 조금 어렵긴 해요. 아직 문화와 언어에 적응하는 중이에요.

👁 **본문 눈으로 이해하기**

Eric : I'm sorry I'm late. I got stuck in traffic.

Ms. Johnson : You're 30 minutes late. This isn't the first time. What happened?

Eric : I'm really sorry, Ms. Johnson. The traffic was worse than usual this morning.

Ms. Johnson : I understand that traffic can be unpredictable, but you need to plan ahead.

Eric : I know, and I take full responsibility. It won't happen again.

Ms. Johnson : I hope so. If this keeps happening, it could affect your performance review.

Eric : I completely understand. I'll make sure to leave earlier from now on.

Ms. Johnson : Good. I appreciate your effort. Now, let's get to work. By the way, have you finished the report I requested?

Eric : Not yet, Ms. Johnson. I sincerely apologize. I was planning to finish it this morning, but since I was late, I couldn't complete it on time.

Ms. Johnson : Eric, this report is important. I need it by the 2 o'clock meeting. Can you have it ready by then?

Eric : Yes, absolutely. I'll make it my top priority and get it done as soon as possible.

43강 사과하기

🗣 본문 소리 내어 읽기

Eric : I'm sorry I'm late. I got stuck in traffic.

Ms. Johnson : You're 30 minutes late. This isn't the first time. What happened?

Eric : I'm really sorry, Ms. Johnson. The traffic was worse than usual / this morning.

Ms. Johnson : I understand that / traffic can be unpredictable, / but you need to plan ahead.

Eric : I know, / and I take full responsibility. It won't happen again.

Ms. Johnson : I hope so. If this keeps happening, / it could affect your performance review.

Eric : I completely understand. I'll make sure to leave earlier / from now on.

Ms. Johnson : Good. I appreciate your effort. Now, let's get to work. By the way, / have you finished the report / I requested?

Eric : Not yet, Ms. Johnson. I sincerely apologize. I was planning to finish it this morning, / but since I was late, / I couldn't complete it on time.

Ms. Johnson : Eric, this report is important. I need it / by the 2 o'clock meeting. Can you have it ready / by then?

Eric : Yes, absolutely. I'll make it my top priority / and get it done / as soon as possible.

43강 사과하기

as A as possible : 가능한 한 A한, A하게

- Can you call me back as soon as possible? It's urgent.

- Please handle this package as carefully as possible. It's very fragile.

- I try to walk as much as possible every day. For example, I often take the stairs instead of the elevator.

43강 사과하기

👄 스피킹2_ 내 이야기해 봅시다

Q Have you said sorry to anyone recently?

A
- I said sorry to my wife for forgetting our wedding anniversary. It was almost a disaster.

- I apologized to a customer for making a mistake. Fortunately, she understood.

- I stepped on someone's foot in the subway and said sorry. I was so embarrassed.

👁 **본문 [해석]**

Eric : 늦어서 죄송합니다. 차가 막혔네요.

Ms. Johnson : 30분 늦었어요. 이번이 처음이 아니에요. 무슨 일이 있었죠?

Eric : 정말 죄송합니다, 존슨씨, 오늘 아침 교통 체증이 평소보다 더 심했어요.

Ms. Johnson : 교통 상황이 예측하기 어렵다는 건 이해하지만, 미리 예상해야 합니다.

Eric : 알고 있습니다. 전적으로 제 책임입니다. 다시는 이런 일이 없을 겁니다.

Ms. Johnson : 그러길 바랍니다. 이런 일이 계속되면 성과 평가에 영향을 미칠 수도 있어요.

Eric : 완전히 이해합니다. 앞으로 반드시 더 일찍 출발하도록 하겠습니다.

Ms. Johnson : 좋아요. 노력하는 모습이 보기 좋네요. 이제 일합시다. 그런데, 요청했던 보고서는 다 끝냈나요?

Eric : 아직 아닙니다, 존슨씨, 진심으로 죄송합니다. 오늘 아침에 완성할 계획이었는데, 늦는 바람에 제시간에 완료하지 못했습니다.

Ms. Johnson : 에릭, 이 보고서는 중요한 자료예요. 오후 2시 회의 전에 필요합니다. 그때까지 준비할 수 있나요?

Eric : 네, 물론입니다. 최우선 순위로 두고 최대한 빨리 끝내겠습니다.

사과하기

👄 스피킹1_ 중요 패턴 익히기 [해석]

as A as possible : 가능한 한 A한, A하게

- 가능한 한 빨리 전화해 줄 수 있나요? 급한 일이에요.

- 이 소포를 가능한 한 조심히 다뤄 주세요. 매우 깨지기 쉬운 물건이에요.

- 나는 매일 가능한 한 많이 걷도록 노력해요. 예를 들어, 나는 엘리베이터 대신 종종 계단을 이용해요.

👄 스피킹2_ 내 이야기해 봅시다 [해석]

질문 최근에 누군가에게 사과해 본 적 있나요?

답
- 나는 결혼기념일을 잊어버려 아내에게 사과했습니다. 거의 재앙이 될 뻔 했어요.

- 나는 고객에게 실수해서 사과했습니다. 다행히 그녀가 이해해 주셨어요.

- 지하철 안에서 다른 사람 발을 밟아 사과했습니다. 너무 창피했어요.

44강 소셜미디어 (SNS)

👁 **본문 눈으로 이해하기**

Social media like Facebook and Instagram are very popular today. They help people stay connected, share their lives, and get information easily. But at the same time, social media has some negative sides.

One advantage of social media is that it helps people communicate. We can talk to friends and family even if they are far away. We can also make new friends and learn about different cultures. Another advantage is that we can get news and useful information quickly. Many people share interesting articles, photos, and videos.

However, social media also has some disadvantages. One problem is that people spend too much time on it. Some people check social media all day and don't focus on their real life. Another problem is that people compare their lives to those of others. On social media, people usually post only the best parts of their lives, like happy moments, vacations, and achievements. Because of this, some people feel unhappy with their own lives.

In conclusion, social media has both good and bad sides. It is useful for communication and information, but we should use it carefully and not spend too much time on it.

44강 소셜미디어 (SNS)

👄 본문 소리 내어 읽기

Social media like Facebook and Instagram / are very popular today. They help people stay connected, / share their lives, / and get information easily. But at the same time, / social media has some negative sides.

One advantage of social media is that / it helps people communicate. We can talk to friends and family / even if they are far away. We can also make new friends / and learn about different cultures. Another advantage is that / we can get news / and useful information quickly. Many people share / interesting articles, photos, and videos.

However, / social media also has some disadvantages. One problem is that / people spend too much time on it. Some people check social media all day / and don't focus on their real life. Another problem is that / people compare their lives / to those of others. On social media, / people usually post / only the best parts of their lives, / like happy moments, vacations, and achievements. Because of this, / some people feel unhappy / with their own lives.

In conclusion, / social media has both good and bad sides. It is useful / for communication and information, / but we should use it carefully / and not spend too much time on it.

44강 소셜미디어 (SNS)

feel happy with : ~에 행복하다, 만족하다
feel unhappy with : ~에 불행하다, 만족하지 않다

- I feel happy with my new home. It's spacious and full of light.

- I feel unhappy with my new haircut. I hope it grows out quickly.

- Do you feel happy with your job, or do you want to try something new?

👄 **스피킹2_ 내 이야기해 봅시다**

Q Do you use social media? If so, which social media app do you use the most?

A ▪ Yes, I do. I mostly use Instagram to stay in touch with friends.

▪ Well, I check Facebook sometimes, but I only browse other people's posts.

▪ Not really. I have an Instagram account, but I don't really use it.

▪ Not at all. I used to use Kakao Story, but I don't anymore.

44강 소셜미디어 (SNS)

◎ 본문 [해석]

소셜 미디어(Facebook 및 Instagram과 같은)는 오늘날 매우 인기가 있습니다. 사람들은 소셜 미디어를 통해 서로 연결된 상태를 유지하고, 자신의 삶을 공유하며, 쉽게 정보를 얻을 수 있습니다. 하지만 동시에, 소셜 미디어에는 부정적인 면도 있습니다.

소셜 미디어의 한 가지 장점은 사람들이 소통할 수 있도록 돕는다는 것입니다. 우리는 멀리 떨어져 있어도 가족 및 친구들과 대화할 수 있습니다. 또한 새로운 친구를 사귀고, 다양한 문화를 배울 수도 있습니다. 또 다른 장점은 뉴스를 빠르게 접하고 유용한 정보를 얻을 수 있다는 것입니다. 많은 사람들이 흥미로운 기사, 사진, 그리고 동영상을 공유합니다.

하지만 소셜 미디어에는 단점도 있습니다. 한 가지 문제는 사람들이 소셜 미디어에 너무 많은 시간을 소비한다는 것입니다. 어떤 사람들은 하루 종일 소셜 미디어를 확인하며 현실 세계에 집중하지 못합니다. 또 다른 문제는 사람들이 자신의 삶을 다른 사람들과 비교한다는 것입니다. 소셜 미디어에서는 주로 행복한 순간, 휴가, 그리고 성취한 일들만 올리는 경우가 많습니다. 그렇기 때문에 일부 사람들은 자신의 삶이 다른 사람들보다 부족하다고 느껴서 불행해질 수 있습니다.

결론적으로, 소셜 미디어에는 좋은 점과 나쁜 점이 모두 있습니다. 소통과 정보 공유에 유용하지만, 우리는 조심해서 사용하고 너무 많은 시간을 소비하지 않도록 해야 합니다.

44강 소셜미디어 (SNS)

feel happy with : ~에 행복하다, 만족하다
feel unhappy with : ~에 불행하다, 만족하지 않다

- 나는 새 집이 마음에 들어. 넓고 채광이 좋아.

- 나는 새 헤어스타일이 마음에 들지 않아. 빨리 자랐으면 좋겠어.

- 너는 지금 직업에 만족해, 아니면 새로운 걸 시도하고 싶어?

👄 **스피킹2_ 내 이야기해 봅시다 [해석]**

질문 소셜 미디어(SNS) 하시나요? 그렇다면 어떤 소셜 미디어 앱을
가장 많이 쓰나요?

답 ■ 응, 그래. 나는 주로 친구들과 연락을 유지하려고 인스타그램
을 사용해.

■ 음, 나는 가끔 페이스북을 확인하지만, 남들이 올린 글만 둘
러봐.

■ 별로 그다지. 인스타그램 계정은 있지만, 거의 사용하지 않아.

■ 전혀 안 써. 예전에는 카카오스토리를 했지만, 이제는 안 해.

45강 감기증상

👁 본문 눈으로 이해하기

Jinsu : Hey Alice, you don't look well. Are you okay?

Alice : Not really. I think I have a cold.

Jinsu : Oh no! What are your symptoms?

Alice : I have a sore throat and a runny nose. But I don't have a fever.

Jinsu : That's good. Have you taken any medicine?

Alice : Yes, I took some medicine. I feel a little better now. What about you? Do you get colds often?

Jinsu : Not really. But when I do, I have body aches and feel really sick. It's terrible.

Alice : That sounds tough. What do you usually do when you catch a cold?

Jinsu : Well, I take medicine and get plenty of rest. Oh, and I make sure to take lots of vitamin C. That helps me recover faster.

Alice : I see. I think I need to take some vitamin C too.

Jinsu : Yeah, it works well for me. I hope you feel better soon!

Alice : Thanks a lot!

👄 **본문 소리 내어 읽기**

Jinsu : Hey Alice, / you don't look well. Are you okay?

Alice : Not really. I think I have a cold.

Jinsu : Oh no! What are your symptoms?

Alice : I have a sore throat / and a runny nose. But I don't have
a fever.

Jinsu : That's good. Have you taken any medicine?

Alice : Yes, I took some medicine. I feel a little better now.
What about you? Do you get colds often?

Jinsu : Not really. But when I do, / I have body aches / and feel
really sick. It's terrible.

Alice : That sounds tough. What do you usually do / when you
catch a cold?

Jinsu : Well, / I take medicine / and get plenty of rest. Oh, and
I make sure / to take lots of vitamin C. That helps me /
recover faster.

Alice : I see. I think / I need to take some vitamin C too.

Jinsu : Yeah, it works well for me. I hope / you feel better soon!

Alice : Thanks a lot!

45강 감기증상

👄 **스피킹1_ 중요 패턴 익히기**

I have + 증상 : 나는 (증상)이 있어

- What are your common symptoms when you catch a cold?

  ➡ I usually have a fever and a sore throat.

✅ **증상명**

No	Symptoms (증상)	English
1	high fever (고열)	I have a high fever.
2	mild fever (미열)	I have a mild fever.
3	chills (오한)	I have chills.
4	headache (두통)	I have a headache.
5	sore throat (인후통)	I have a sore throat.
6	cough (기침)	I have a cough.
7	runny nose (콧물)	I have a runny nose.
8	stuffy nose (코막힘)	I have a stuffy nose.
9	body aches (몸살)	I have body aches.
10	phlegm (가래)	I have phlegm.

💋 스피킹2_ 내 이야기해 봅시다

Q Have you had a cold recently? If so, what were your symptoms?

A
- Yes, I caught a bad cold last week, and I had a runny and stuffy nose. It was really tough.

- Yes, I suffered from the flu last month. I had a high fever and chills, so I had to get an IV drip.

- No, not recently. I guess I've been lucky. The cold going around these days is really bad.

👁 본문 [해석]

Jinsu : 앨리스, 안 좋아 보이는데 괜찮아?

Alice : 별로 안 괜찮아. 감기 걸린 것 같아.

Jinsu : 아, 안됐네! 증상이 뭐야?

Alice : 목이 아프고 콧물이 나. 근데 열은 없어.

Jinsu : 그나마 다행이네. 약은 먹었어?

Alice : 응, 약을 먹었어. 좀 나아진 것 같아.

　　　너는 어때? 감기 자주 걸려?

Jinsu : 별로 안 걸려. 근데 한 번 걸리면 몸살도 나고 엄청 아파. 진짜 힘들어.

Alice : 힘들겠다. 감기 걸리면 보통 어떻게 해?

Jinsu : 음, 약 먹고 푹 쉬어. 아, 그리고 비타민 C도 꼭 챙겨 먹어. 그러면 더 빨리 나아지더라.

Alice : 그렇구나. 나도 비타민 C 좀 챙겨 먹어야겠다.

Jinsu : 응, 나한테는 효과가 좋아. 얼른 나아!

Alice : 고마워!

45강 감기증상

🗣 스피킹1_ 중요 패턴 익히기 [해석]

I have + 증상 : 나는 (증상)이 있어

- 감기 걸렸을 때 당신의 흔한 증상은 무엇인가요?

  ➡ 나는 주로 열이 나고, 목이 아파요.

⊘ 증상명 [해석]

No	Symptoms (증상)	English
1	high fever (고열)	나는 고열이 있어.
2	mild fever (미열)	나는 미열이 있어.
3	chills (오한)	나는 오한이 있어.
4	headache (두통)	나는 두통이 있어.
5	sore throat (인후통)	나는 목이 아파.
6	cough (기침)	나는 기침이 나.
7	runny nose (콧물)	나는 콧물이 나.
8	stuffy nose (코막힘)	나는 코가 막혀.
9	body aches (몸살)	나는 몸살이 있어.
10	phlegm (가래)	나는 가래가 있어.

🗣️ 스피킹2_ 내 이야기해 봅시다 [해석]

질문 최근에 감기에 걸린 적 있나요? 그렇다면 증상이 뭐였나요?

답
- 네, 지난주에 심한 감기에 걸렸어요. 콧물이 나고, 코가 막혔어요. 정말 힘들었어요.

- 네, 지난달에 독감에 걸렸어요. 고열과 오한이 있어서 수액을 맞아야 했어요.

- 아니요, 최근에는 감기 안 걸렸어요. 운이 좋았던 것 같아요. 요즘 돌고 있는 감기 정말 독해요.

MEMO

◎ **본문 눈으로 이해하기**

(Q) Have you ever had a part-time job?

Yes, I have had a part-time job before. When I was in my twenties, I worked at a coffee shop. I love coffee, so I wanted to learn how to make it. While working there, I learned a lot about coffee, and I also realized that I enjoy customer service. I'm an outgoing and social person, so I liked talking to people and serving them. It was a great experience for me.

Later, after getting married and having children, I wanted to earn some extra money in my free time. So, after my kids grew up a bit, I started working at a convenience store. I work from 10 a.m. to 3 p.m. on weekdays while my kids are at school. My boss understands my situation and lets me work flexible hours, which I really appreciate. My job includes handling the cash register, organizing products, and checking expired items. It can be tiring, but I feel happy that I can use my free time to earn money.

👄 **본문 소리 내어 읽기**

(Q) Have you ever had a part-time job?

Yes, / I have had a part-time job before. When I was in my twenties, / I worked at a coffee shop. I love coffee, / so I wanted to learn / how to make it. While working there, / I learned a lot about coffee, / and I also realized / that I enjoy customer service. I'm an outgoing and social person, / so I liked talking to people / and serving them. It was a great experience for me.

Later, / after getting married / and having children, I wanted to earn some extra money / in my free time. So, / after my kids grew up a bit, / I started working / at a convenience store. I work from 10 a.m. to 3 p.m. on weekdays / while my kids are at school. My boss understands my situation / and lets me work flexible hours, / which I really appreciate. My job includes handling the cash register, / organizing products, / and checking expired items. It can be tiring, / but I feel happy / that I can use my free time / to earn money.

아르바이트

👄 스피킹1_ 중요 패턴 익히기

let A + 동사원형 : A가 (동사)하게 허락하다

- My father lets me use his car, but I have to pay for the gas.

- My mother didn't let me drink coffee when I was a child.

- Just let them do it. They're all grown up now.

- Just let it go. It's not a big deal.

46강 아르바이트

😊 **스피킹2_ 내 이야기해 봅시다**

Q **Have you ever had a part-time job?**

A
- Yes, I used to work at a restaurant. It was quite hard, but I learned a lot from it.

- Yes, I worked at a construction site. It was physically tough, but the pay was good.

- Well, I have a part-time job now. I'm delivering food in my free time after work.

- No, I haven't. I've never had a part-time job before.

👁 본문 [해석]

(질문) 아르바이트를 해 본 적 있나요?

네, 저는 전에 아르바이트를 한 적이 있습니다. 제가 20대였을 때, 커피숍에서 일했어요. 저는 커피를 좋아해서 커피 만드는 법을 배우고 싶었어요. 그곳에서 일하면서 커피에 대해 많은 것을 배웠고, 고객 서비스를 즐긴다는 것도 깨달았어요. 저는 외향적이고 사교적인 성격이라서 사람들과 이야기하고 그들을 응대하는 것이 즐거웠어요. 저에게는 좋은 경험이었습니다.

나중에 결혼하고 아이를 낳은 후, 여가 시간에 추가로 돈을 벌고 싶었어요. 그래서 아이들이 어느 정도 자란 뒤에 편의점에서 일하기 시작했어요. 저는 평일 오전 10시부터 오후 3시까지 아이들이 학교에 있는 동안 일해요. 제 사장님은 제 상황을 이해해 주시고, 유연한 근무 시간을 허락해 주셔서 정말 감사하게 생각해요. 제 일은 계산대 업무, 상품 정리 및 진열, 그리고 유통기한이 지난 제품을 확인하는 것입니다. 가끔 힘들 때도 있지만, 저는 남는 시간을 활용해서 돈을 벌 수 있다는 점에서 만족감을 느낍니다.

👄 스피킹1_ 중요 패턴 익히기 [해석]

let A + 동사원형 : A가 (동사)하게 허락하다

- 아버지가 나에게 차를 쓰게 해 주시지만, 나는 기름값을 내야 해.

- 어렸을 때, 어머니는 내가 커피를 마시지 못하게 하셨다.

- 그냥 걔네가 하게 둬. 이제 다 컸잖아.

- 그냥 흘려버려. 별일 아니야.

👄 스피킹2_ 내 이야기해 봅시다 [해석]

질문 혹시 아르바이트를 해 본 적 있나요?

답 ■ 네, 저는 예전에 레스토랑에서 일했어요. 꽤 힘들었지만, 많은 것을 배웠어요.

■ 네, 저는 공사 현장에서 일했어요. 육체적으로 힘들었지만, 보수가 좋았어요.

■ 음, 지금 저는 아르바이트를 하고 있어요. 퇴근 후 여가 시간에 음식 배달을 하고 있어요.

■ 아니요, 저는 한 번도 아르바이트를 해 본 적이 없어요.

 **47강** 물건 찾기

◉ 본문 **눈으로 이해하기**

Husband : Honey, have you seen my car key? I can't find it anywhere.

Wife : Hmm... Did you check your pockets?

Husband : Yes, I checked my jacket and jeans. It's not there.

Wife : Where did you last see it?

Husband : I remember locking the car with it.

Wife : Okay, then you must have brought it inside.

Husband : Yeah, but I don't remember where I put it.

Wife : Maybe it's on the table?

Husband : No, I already looked there.

Wife : How about the sofa? You were watching TV there earlier, right?

Husband : Oh, right! Let me check... *(looks under the cushions)* Ah-ha! Found it!

Wife : Where was it?

Husband : Under the sofa cushion. I must have dropped it when I was watching TV earlier. It probably fell out of my pocket.

Wife : I knew it! Next time, check the sofa first.

Husband : Yeah, I should. Thanks!

👄 본문 소리 내어 읽기

Husband : Honey, **/** have you seen my car key? I can't find it anywhere.

Wife : Hmm... Did you check your pockets?

Husband : Yes, I checked my jacket and jeans. It's not there.

Wife : Where did you last see it?

Husband : I remember **/** locking the car with it.

Wife : Okay, **/** then you must have brought it inside.

Husband : Yeah, **/** but I don't remember **/** where I put it.

Wife : Maybe it's on the table?

Husband : No, I already looked there.

Wife : How about the sofa? You were watching TV there **/** earlier, right?

Husband : Oh, right! Let me check... *(looks under the cushions)* Ah-ha! Found it!

Wife : Where was it?

Husband : Under the sofa cushion. I must have dropped it **/** when I was watching TV earlier. It probably **/** fell out of my pocket.

Wife : I knew it! Next time, **/** check the sofa first.

Husband : Yeah, I should. Thanks!

스피킹1_ 중요 패턴 익히기

must have p.p (동사의 과거분사형) : 했음이 분명해
→ 과거에 대한 강한 추측

- I must have left my phone at home. Can you call my number and check?

- You must have been shocked! What did you do after that?

- He must have been tired. He kept dozing off.

- This must have been really expensive. Where did you get it?

47강 물건 찾기

Q **Have you ever lost something important?**

A ■ Of course. I lost my wallet last year. I had to cancel all my cards.

■ Yes, I lost my wedding ring once, but luckily, I found it later.

■ Yes, I lost my phone while traveling abroad. I think someone took it.

■ No, I've never lost anything important. I'm pretty careful.

👁 본문 [해석]

남편 : 자기야, 내 차 키 봤어? 어디에도 없어.

아내 : 음... 주머니 확인해 봤어?

남편 : 응, 재킷이랑 청바지 다 확인했어. 거기엔 없어.

아내 : 마지막으로 어디에서 봤어?

남편 : 차 문을 잠글 때 본 것 같아.

아내 : 그럼 집 안으로 가지고 들어왔겠네.

남편 : 응, 그런데 어디에 뒀는지 기억이 안 나.

아내 : 테이블 위에 있을지도 몰라.

남편 : 아니, 거기는 이미 찾아봤어.

아내 : 소파는 어때? 아까 소파에서 TV 봤잖아, 맞지?

남편 : 아, 맞다! 한 번 확인해 볼게... *(쿠션을 들춰본다)*

　　　 아하! 찾았어!

아내 : 어디 있었어?

남편 : 소파 쿠션 밑에 있었어. 아까 TV 볼 때 떨어졌나 보다. 아마 주머니

　　　 에서 빠진 것 같아.

아내 : 그럴 줄 알았어! 다음엔 먼저 소파부터 확인해 봐.

남편 : 그래야겠다. 고마워!

물건 찾기

👄 스피킹1_ 중요 패턴 익히기 [해석]

must have p.p (동사의 과거분사형) : 했음이 분명해

➡️ 과거에 대한 강한 추측

- 내 폰을 집에 두고 왔나 봐. 내 번호로 전화 걸어서 확인해 줄 수 있어?

- 너 엄청 놀랐겠네! 그리고 나서 어떻게 했어?

- 그 사람 엄청 피곤했나 봐. 계속 졸더라.

- 이거 정말 비쌌겠다. 어디서 샀어?

👄 스피킹2_ 내 이야기해 봅시다 [해석]

질문 혹시 중요한 뭔가를 잃어버린 적이 있어?

답
- 물론이야. 작년에 지갑을 잃어버렸어. 모든 카드를 정지시켜야 했어.

- 응, 결혼반지를 한 번 잃어버렸었어. 하지만 다행히 나중에 찾았어.

- 응, 해외여행 중에 핸드폰을 잃어버렸어. 누군가 가져간 것 같아.

- 아니, 중요한 걸 잃어버린 적은 한 번도 없어. 나는 꽤 조심하는 편이야.

48강 우리 동네

◉ 본문 **눈으로 이해하기**

<My Neighborhood>

I live in Yongin, and I've been here for ten years since I got married. My home is about a 15-minute walk from the subway station, and there are a few buses, so it's easy to get around.

One thing I really like about my neighborhood is that there's an elementary school nearby. As a parent, it's nice to have a school close to home. But what I love about my neighborhood is the public library. It's within walking distance, so on weekends, I enjoy going there with my kids.

Of course, there are a few downsides. My neighborhood is on a bit of a hill, so when it snows a lot in winter, it can be difficult to get around. But on the bright side, the view from my house is amazing. Another small inconvenience is that there isn't a large supermarket within walking distance, so I usually drive when I go grocery shopping.

Still, I really like my neighborhood. It's peaceful and quiet, and most of the people here are kind and polite. Unless something special happens, I'd love to live here for a long time.

48강 우리 동네

😙 본문 소리 내어 읽기

<My Neighborhood>

I live in Yongin, / and I've been here for ten years / since I got married. My home is about a 15-minute walk / from the subway station, / and there are a few buses, / so it's easy to get around.

One thing / I really like about my neighborhood / is that there's an elementary school nearby. As a parent, / it's nice to have a school / close to home. But what I love about my neighborhood / is the public library. It's within walking distance, / so on weekends, / I enjoy going there with my kids.

Of course, / there are a few downsides. My neighborhood is on a bit of a hill, / so when it snows a lot in winter, / it can be difficult to get around. But on the bright side, / the view from my house is amazing. Another small inconvenience / is that there isn't a large supermarket / within walking distance, / so I usually drive / when I go grocery shopping.

Still, / I really like my neighborhood. It's peaceful and quiet, / and most of the people here / are kind and polite. Unless something special happens, / I'd love to live here / for a long time.

🗣 스피킹1_ 중요 패턴 익히기

what I love about A is ~ : 내가 A에 대해 아주 좋아하는 것은 ~이다

- What I love about autumn is the colorful leaves. You can see them anywhere in Korea.

- What I love about Jeonju is the delicious food. It's the best place to enjoy authentic Korean food.

- What I love about my best friend is that she always listens to me. She's very caring and understanding.

48강 우리 동네

👄 스피킹2_ 내 이야기해 봅시다

Q What do you like about your neighborhood?

A
- There are many parks and green spaces, so it's a great place to take a walk.

- There are schools nearby, so it's a great place to raise children.

- I like that it's close to the subway, so getting around is really easy.

- I like that it's quiet and peaceful, so life here is more relaxing.

우리 동네

◎ **본문 [해석]**

나는 용인에 살고 있고, 결혼한 후 10년 동안 이곳에서 살고 있다. 우리 집은 지하철역에서 걸어서 약 15분 거리에 있으며, 버스도 몇 대 있어서 교통이 편리하다.

내가 우리 동네에서 정말 좋아하는 것 중 하나는 근처에 초등학교가 있다는 점이다. 부모로서 학교가 가까이에 있는 것은 정말 좋은 일이다. 하지만 우리 동네에 관해 내가 가장 좋아하는 것은 공공 도서관이다. 걸어갈 수 있는 거리에 있어서, 주말에는 아이들과 함께 도서관에 가는 것을 즐긴다.

물론 단점도 몇 가지 있다. 우리 동네는 약간 언덕 위에 있어서, 겨울에 눈이 많이 내리면 다니기가 어렵다. 하지만 좋은 점도 있는데, 우리 집에서 바라보는 전망이 정말 멋지다. 또 하나의 작은 불편함은 걸어서 갈 수 있는 큰 마트가 없다는 점이다. 그래서 나는 주로 차를 타고 장을 보러 간다.

그럼에도 불구하고 나는 우리 동네가 정말 마음에 든다. 조용하고 평화로우며, 대부분의 사람들이 친절하고 예의 바르다. 특별한 일이 없는 한, 나는 이곳에서 오랫동안 살고 싶다.

우리 동네

👄 스피킹1_ 중요 패턴 익히기 [해석]

what I love about A is ~ : 내가 A에 대해 아주 좋아하는 것은 ~이다

- 내가 가을에 대해 아주 좋아하는 것은 알록달록한 단풍이야. 한국 어디에서나 그것들을 볼 수 있어.

- 내가 전주에 대해 아주 좋아하는 것은 맛있는 음식이야. 전주는 정통 한식을 즐기기에 최고의 장소야.

- 내가 내 절친에 대해 아주 좋아하는 것은 그녀가 항상 내 말을 잘 들어준다는 거야. 그녀는 정말 다정하고 이해심이 많아.

👄 스피킹2_ 내 이야기해 봅시다 [해석]

질문 너의 동네 뭐가 마음에 들어?

답
- 공원과 녹지가 많아서, 산책하기 좋은 곳이야.

- 근처에 학교들이 있어서, 아이들 키우기에 좋은 곳이야.

- 지하철이 가까워서 좋아. 그래서 이동하기가 정말 편리해.

- 조용하고 평화로워서 좋아. 그래서 여기 삶은 좀 더 여유로워.

49강 약속 잡기

👁 본문 눈으로 이해하기

Alice : Hey Jinsu! Do you have any plans this weekend?

Jinsu : Hi Alice! Not yet. Do you want to hang out?

Alice : Yes! That sounds great. When are you free?

Jinsu : Hmm... How about Saturday afternoon?

Alice : Saturday afternoon works for me! What time should we meet?

Jinsu : Maybe around 2 p.m.?

Alice : Well, I'm not sure if I can make it at 2. I have lunch plans. How about 3 p.m.?

Jinsu : No problem! Is there anywhere you want to go?

Alice : Actually, I want to go to Insadong. I haven't been there yet.

Jinsu : Oh, really? Insadong is a great place! You can find lots of traditional Korean items there.

Alice : Yeah, I heard that too. I want to go buy some souvenirs for my family in the States.

Jinsu : And let's have tea at a traditional tea house. There are many good ones there.

Alice : Great! Where should we meet?

Jinsu : Let's meet at Anguk Station, Exit 6, on Subway Line 3. From there, we can walk straight to Insadong Street.

Alice : Sounds perfect. I can't wait! See you there!

👄 본문 소리 내어 읽기

Alice : Hey Jinsu! Do you have any plans this weekend?

Jinsu : Hi Alice! Not yet. Do you want to hang out?

Alice : Yes! That sounds great. When are you free?

Jinsu : Hmm... How about Saturday afternoon?

Alice : Saturday afternoon works for me! What time should we meet?

Jinsu : Maybe around 2 p.m.?

Alice : Well, I'm not sure / if I can make it at 2. I have lunch plans. How about 3 p.m.?

Jinsu : No problem! Is there anywhere / you want to go?

Alice : Actually, / I want to go to Insadong. I haven't been there yet.

Jinsu : Oh, really? Insadong is a great place! You can find lots of traditional Korean items there.

Alice : Yeah, I heard that too. I want to go buy some souvenirs / for my family in the States.

Jinsu : And let's have tea / at a traditional tea house. There are many good ones there.

Alice : Great! Where should we meet?

Jinsu : Let's meet at Anguk Station, / Exit 6, / on Subway Line 3. From there, / we can walk straight / to Insadong Street.

Alice : Sounds perfect. I can't wait! See you there!

약속 잡기

👄 **스피킹1_ 중요 패턴 익히기**

> **I'm not sure if** 주어 + 동사 : ~인지 아닌지 잘 모르겠어

- I'm not sure if I can make it tomorrow. Something came up.

- I'm not sure if he's coming. He hasn't replied yet.

- I'm not sure if she'll like it. She's quite picky.

- I'm not sure if this is the right way. Let's ask someone.

👄 **스피킹2_ 내 이야기해 봅시다**

> **Q** Do you usually have a lot of plans?

A
- Yes, my schedule is usually packed. I'm always busy with work, family gatherings, and social events.

- Not much. I usually just go with the flow. I don't like making too many plans.

- Sometimes I do, sometimes I don't. It depends on the situation.

약속 잡기

👁 본문 [해석]

Alice : 진수야! 주말에 계획 있어?

Jinsu : 안녕, 앨리스! 아직 없어. 같이 놀래?

Alice : 응! 너무 좋지. 언제 시간이 돼?

Jinsu : 음... 토요일 오후 어때?

Alice : 토요일 오후 괜찮아! 몇 시에 만날까?

Jinsu : 오후 2시쯤 어때?

Alice : 음, 2시에 갈 수 있을지 잘 모르겠어. 점심 약속이 있어. 3시는 어때?

Jinsu : 괜찮아! 가고 싶은 곳 있어?

Alice : 사실 인사동에 가고 싶어. 아직 한 번도 안 가봤어.

Jinsu : 아, 정말? 인사동 좋은 곳이야! 거기서 다양한 한국 전통 물건들을 살 수 있어.

Alice : 응, 나도 그렇게 들었어. 미국에 있는 가족들에게 줄 기념품을 사고 싶어서 가고 싶었어.

Jinsu : 그리고 전통 찻집에서 차도 마시자. 좋은 찻집이 많아.

Alice : 좋아! 어디서 만날까?

Jinsu : 지하철 3호선 안국역 6번 출구에서 만나자. 거기서 바로 걸어가면 인사동 거리야.

Alice : 완벽해! 기대돼! 거기서 보자!

49강 약속 잡기

👄 스피킹1_ 중요 패턴 익히기 [해석]

I'm not sure if 주어 + 동사 : ~인지 아닌지 잘 모르겠어

- 내일 갈 수 있을지 모르겠어. 갑자기 일이 생겼어.

- 그가 올지 모르겠어. 아직 답장을 안 했어.

- 그녀가 좋아할지 모르겠어. 그녀는 꽤 까다로운 편이야.

- 이게 맞는 길인지 모르겠어. 누군가에게 물어보자.

👄 스피킹2_ 내 이야기해 봅시다 [해석]

질문 보통 약속이 많은 편이야?

답
- 응, 내 일정은 보통 꽉 차 있어. 나는 항상 일, 가족 모임, 그리고 사적인 모임으로 바빠.

- 별로 없어. 그냥 흐름대로 지내. 약속 많이 잡는 거 안 좋아해.

- 어떤 때는 그렇고, 어떤 때는 안 그래. 상황에 따라 다르지.

50강 길 물어보기

Guest : Excuse me, I'd like to visit Times Square. Could you tell me how to get there?

Front Desk Agent : Of course! Let me show you on the map. We are here at the hotel, and Times Square is over here. There are a few ways to get there.

If you'd like to walk, it takes about 15 minutes from here. Just step out of the hotel and turn right. Walk straight along 7th Avenue for about 10 blocks, and you'll see Times Square on your right. It's hard to miss!

You can also take a bus if you prefer. The nearest bus stop is just one block away. Step out of the hotel and turn left. Take bus number M7 and get off at West 42nd Street. From there, it's just a 2-minute walk to Times Square.

Or, if you'd like, I can call a taxi for you. It'll take about 5 minutes, depending on traffic. Would you like me to call one for you now?

Guest : No, thank you. I think I'll walk. Thank you so much for your help!

Front Desk Agent : You're very welcome! Here, take this map with you. Enjoy your visit to Times Square!

👄 본문 소리 내어 읽기

Guest : Excuse me, **/** I'd like to visit Times Square. Could you tell me **/** how to get there?

Front Desk Agent : Of course! Let me show you **/** on the map. We are here at the hotel, **/** and Times Square is over here. There are a few ways to get there.

If you'd like to walk, **/** it takes about 15 minutes from here. Just step out of the hotel, **/** and turn right. Walk straight **/** along 7th Avenue **/** for about 10 blocks, **/** and you'll see Times Square **/** on your right. It's hard to miss!

You can also take a bus **/** if you prefer. The nearest bus stop **/** is just one block away. Step out of the hotel, **/** and turn left. Take bus number M7, **/** and get off at West 42nd Street. From there, **/** it's just a 2-minute walk **/** to Times Square.

Or, **/** if you'd like, **/** I can call a taxi for you. It'll take about 5 minutes, **/** depending on traffic. Would you like me to call one **/** for you now?

Guest : No, thank you. I think I'll walk. Thank you so much **/** for your help!

Front Desk Agent : You're very welcome! Here, **/** take this map with you. Enjoy your visit **/** to Times Square!

👄 **스피킹1_ 중요 패턴 익히기**

Would you like me to 동사원형 : 제가 ~ 해 드릴까요?

- Would you like me to help you with your luggage?

  → Yes, please.

  → Thank you. This is for you. (가방 1개당 1-2달러 정도)

- Would you like me to refill your water?

  → Yes, please. Thank you.

  → No, thank you. I'm good for now.

- Would you like me to take your plates now?

  → Yes, that would be great.

  → No, thank you. I'm still eating.

- Would you like me to bring the check now?

  → Yes, please. We're done.

  → No, thank you. We're still enjoying our meal.

50강 길 물어보기

👄 **스피킹2_ 내 이야기해 봅시다**

Q **Have you asked for directions recently?**

A
- Yes, I have. I got lost last week and had to ask someone.

- Yes, I have. Google Maps wasn't working, so I had to ask someone.

- No, I haven't. I usually use my phone for directions.

- No, I haven't. I'm pretty good with directions.

길 물어보기

◎ **본문 [해석]**

손님: 실례합니다. 타임스 스퀘어에 가고 싶은데, 어떻게 가는지 알려 주실 수 있나요?

호텔 직원: 물론이죠! 지도로 보여드릴게요. 저희 호텔이 여기 있고, 타임스 스퀘어는 이쪽이에요. 가는 방법이 몇 가지 있습니다.

걸어서 가신다면 여기서 약 15분 정도 걸립니다. 그냥 호텔을 나가서 오른쪽으로 도세요. 7번가를 따라 약 10블록 정도 직진하시면 됩니다. 그러면 오른쪽에 타임스 스퀘어가 보일 거예요. 찾기 쉬워요!

버스를 이용하실 수도 있습니다. 가장 가까운 버스 정류장은 한 블록 거리에 있어요. 호텔을 나가서 왼쪽으로 가세요. M7번 버스를 타고 West 42nd Street에서 내리시면 됩니다. 거기서 타임스 스퀘어까지는 도보로 2분밖에 걸리지 않아요.

또는, 원하시면 택시를 불러 드릴 수도 있어요. 교통 상황에 따라 다르지만 약 5분 정도 걸릴 거예요. 제가 지금 불러드릴까요?

손님: 아니요, 괜찮습니다. 걸어가기로 할게요. 도와주셔서 정말 감사합니다!

호텔 직원: 천만에요! 여기 지도 가져가세요. 타임스 스퀘어에서 즐거운 시간 보내세요!

🫦 스피킹1_ 중요 패턴 익히기 [해석]

Would you like me to 동사원형 : 제가 ~ 해 드릴까요?

- 제가 짐 들어 드릴까요?

  ➡ 네, 부탁드려요.

  ➡ 감사합니다. 이거 받아주세요.

- 물 리필해 드릴까요?

  ➡ 네, 부탁드려요. 감사합니다.

  ➡ 아니요, 괜찮아요. 지금은 충분해요.

- 접시 치워 드릴까요?

  ➡ 네, 그러면 좋겠어요.

  ➡ 아니요, 괜찮아요. 아직 먹고 있어요.

- 지금 계산서 가져다 드릴까요?

  ➡ 네, 부탁드려요. 저희 다 먹었습니다.

  ➡ 아니요, 괜찮아요. 아직 식사 중이에요.

50강 길 물어보기

스피킹2_ 내 이야기해 봅시다 [해석]

질문 최근에 길을 물어본 적이 있나요?

답
- 네, 있어요. 지난주에 길을 잃어서 누군가에게 물어봐야 했어요.

- 네, 있어요. 구글 맵이 작동하지 않아서 누군가에게 물어봐야 했어요.

- 아니요, 없어요. 저는 보통 휴대폰으로 길을 찾아요.

- 아니요, 없어요. 저는 길 찾는 걸 꽤 잘해요.

MEMO

 **51강** 길 알려주기

👁 본문 눈으로 이해하기

Jinsu : Excuse me, do you need any help?

Foreigner : Oh, yes, please! I want to go to Bukchon Hanok Village, but I think I'm going the wrong way.

Jinsu : I see. Which exit did you use at Anguk Station?

Foreigner : I'm not sure.

Jinsu : No problem. This way leads to Jongno 3-ga, but Bukchon Hanok Village is in the opposite direction. You need to take Exit 2.

Foreigner : Oh! So should I go back to the station and use Exit 2?

Jinsu : Yes, that would be easier. But if you don't want to go back, just turn around and walk straight until you reach the station entrance again. Instead of going inside, cross the street and keep walking straight. After two blocks, you'll see Jaedong Elementary School on your right. Turn right there, and you'll find the road leading to Bukchon Hanok Village.

Foreigner : Got it! Thank you so much for your help.

Jinsu : You're welcome! Enjoy your time in Seoul!

👄 본문 소리 내어 읽기

Jinsu : Excuse me, **/** do you need any help?

Foreigner : Oh, yes, please! I want to go to Bukchon Hanok Village, **/** but I think I'm going the wrong way.

Jinsu : I see. Which exit did you use **/** at Anguk Station?

Foreigner : I'm not sure.

Jinsu : No problem. This way leads to Jongno 3-ga, **/** but Bukchon Hanok Village **/** is in the opposite direction. You need to take Exit 2.

Foreigner : Oh! So should I go back to the station, **/** and use Exit 2?

Jinsu : Yes, that would be easier. But if you don't want to go back, **/** just turn around, **/** and walk straight **/** until you reach the station entrance again. Instead of going inside, **/** cross the street, **/** and keep walking straight. After two blocks, **/** you'll see Jaedong Elementary School **/** on your right. Turn right there, **/** and you'll find the road leading to Bukchon Hanok Village.

Foreigner : Got it! Thank you so much **/** for your help.

Jinsu : You're welcome! Enjoy your time in Seoul!

길 알려주기

🗣️ **스피킹1_ 중요 패턴 익히기**

Should I 동사원형 : 제가 (동사)하는 게 좋을까요?
➡ (상대방의 의견을 구할 때)

- Should I get the beige one or the khaki one? I can't decide!

- Should I change my outfit? Is this too casual?

- Should I pick you up, or are you taking the bus?

👄 **스피킹2_ 내 이야기해 봅시다**

외국인에게 길을 알려줄 때 질문하기

- Excuse me, do you need any help?

해외에서 길을 물을 때 질문하기

- Excuse me, I'd like to go to (COEX   ).

  Could you tell me how to get there?

길 알려주기

🗨️ **스피킹2_ 내 이야기해 봅시다**

1. 지하철로 알려줄 때

- 오이도행 4호선을 타고 사당역에서 내린 뒤, 잠실 방향 2호선으로 갈아타세요. 삼성역에서 내린 뒤, 6번 출구 쪽으로 가면 코엑스가 나옵니다.

→ Take Line 4 toward Oido and get off at Sadang Station. Then, transfer to Line 2 toward Jamsil. Get off at Samseong Station, and head toward Exit 6. You will find COEX there.

2. 버스로 알려줄 때

- 저기 저쪽에 버스 정류장이 있어. 143번 혹은 2413번 버스를 타고 한 20분 정도 가서 코엑스아티움에서 내려. 그럼 근처에 코엑스몰이 바로 보일 거야.

→ There's a bus stop over there. Take bus 143 or 2413, and stay on the bus for about 20 minutes. Get off at COEX Artium, and COEX Mall will be nearby.

3. 도보로 알려줄 때

- 삼성역 4번 출구로 나와서 두 블록 쭉 직진한 뒤 좌회전해. 다시 쭉 한 블록 가서 길을 건너면, 왼쪽에 이비스 호텔이 보일 거야.

→ Take Exit 4 at Samseong Station, then go straight for two blocks and turn left. Walk one more block straight, then cross the street. You'll see the Ibis Hotel on your left.

👁 **본문 [해석]**

Jinsu : 실례합니다. 도움이 필요하신가요?

외국인 : 오, 네! 저는 북촌 한옥마을에 가고 싶은데, 잘못 가고 있는 것 같아요.

Jinsu : 그렇군요. 안국역에서 어느 출구로 나오셨어요?

외국인 : 잘 모르겠어요.

Jinsu : 괜찮아요. 이 길은 종로 3가 방향으로 가는 길인데, 북촌 한옥마을은 반대 방향이에요. 2번 출구로 나가셔야 해요.

외국인 : 오! 그러면 다시 역으로 돌아가서 2번 출구로 나가야 하나요?

Jinsu : 네, 그렇게 하는 게 더 쉬울 거예요. 하지만 역으로 돌아가고 싶지 않다면, 그냥 뒤돌아서 곧장 걸어가세요. 그러면 다시 역 입구에 도착할 거예요. 그때 역 안으로 들어가지 말고 길을 건너서 계속 직진하세요. 두 블록 지나면 오른쪽에 재동초등학교가 보일 거예요. 거기에서 우회전하면 북촌 한옥마을로 가는 길이 나올 거예요.

외국인 : 알겠어요! 도와주셔서 정말 감사합니다.

Jinsu : 천만에요! 서울에서 좋은 시간 보내세요!

길 알려주기

🫦 스피킹1_ 중요 패턴 익히기 [해석]

Should I 동사원형 : 제가 (동사)하는 게 좋을까요?
→ (상대방의 의견을 구할 때)

- 베이지색을 살까, 카키색을 살까? 결정을 못 하겠어!

- 옷을 갈아입는 게 좋을까? 이거 너무 캐주얼한가?

- 내가 데리러 갈까, 아니면 버스 탈 거야?

길 알려주기

👄 **스피킹2_ 내 이야기해 봅시다 [해석]**

외국인에게 길을 알려줄 때 질문하기

- 실례합니다. 도움이 필요하세요?

해외에서 길을 물을 때 질문하기

- 실례합니다. (　코엑스　)에 가고 싶은데, 어떻게 가는지 알려줄 수 있나요?

길 알려주기

1. 지하철로 알려줄 때

- 오이도행 4호선을 타고 사당역에서 내린 뒤, 잠실 방향 2호선으로 갈아타세요. 삼성역에서 내린 뒤, 6번 출구 쪽으로 가면 코엑스가 나옵니다.

2. 버스로 알려줄 때

- 저기 저쪽에 버스 정류장이 있어. 143번 혹은 2413번 버스를 타고 한 20분 정도 가서 코엑스아티움에서 내려. 그럼 근처에 코엑스몰이 바로 보일 거야.

3. 도보로 알려줄 때

- 삼성역 4번 출구로 나와서 두 블록 쭉 직진한 뒤 좌회전해. 다시 쭉 한 블록 가서 길을 건너면, 왼쪽에 이비스 호텔이 보일 거야.

◉ **본문 눈으로 이해하기**

I watch YouTube a lot for two reasons.

First, I can learn many things from it. Many experts and regular people share their knowledge and skills for free. I even learned to play the guitar by watching YouTube videos, and it helped me a lot.

Second, I can find helpful tips for daily life. I can learn cooking recipes, exercise routines, and ways to save money. For example, every time I cook dinner, I watch my favorite cooking YouTube channel, choose a menu, and follow the recipe.

But I think YouTube also has some downsides. There was a time when I watched YouTube too much, and it affected my focus at work and my sleep at night.

Another problem is YouTube Shorts. These short videos are very addictive, so it's easy to waste time watching them without thinking.

In conclusion, YouTube is a very useful platform for learning and getting information, but I need to be careful not to get addicted. I should use it wisely and try to balance it with real life.

본문 소리 내어 읽기

I watch YouTube a lot / for two reasons.

First, / I can learn many things from it. Many experts and regular people / share their knowledge and skills / for free. I even learned to play the guitar / by watching YouTube videos, / and it helped me a lot.

Second, / I can find helpful tips / for daily life. I can learn cooking recipes, / exercise routines, / and ways to save money. For example, / every time I cook dinner, / I watch my favorite cooking YouTube channel, / choose a menu, / and follow the recipe.

But I think / YouTube also has some downsides. There was a time / when I watched YouTube too much, / and it affected my focus at work / and my sleep at night.

Another problem is YouTube Shorts. These short videos are very addictive, / so it's easy to waste time / watching them without thinking.

In conclusion, / YouTube is a very useful platform / for learning and getting information, / but I need to be careful / not to get addicted. I should use it wisely / and try to balance it / with real life.

There was a time when I 동사과거형

: (동사)했던 때가 있었다, 한때 (동사)했었다

- There was a time when I wanted to be a singer, but now I just sing as a hobby.

- There was a time when I drank too much, but now I drink just a little.

- There was a time when I went on a strict diet, but now I focus more on my health.

52강 유튜브

👄 **스피킹2_ 내 이야기해 봅시다**

Q Do you often watch YouTube? If so, what's your favorite YouTube channel?

A
- Yes, I watch YouTube almost every day, and I especially love travel channels like "Pani Bottle".

- Yes, I watch it a lot, especially before bed at night. My favorite channel is "Korean Englishman". It's hilarious.

- Sometimes I do, sometimes I don't. I don't have a favorite channel, but I enjoy watching movie channels.

52강 유튜브

👁 본문 [해석]

나는 두 가지 이유 때문에 유튜브를 많이 본다.

첫째, 유튜브에서 많은 것을 배울 수 있다. 많은 전문가와 일반 사람들이 자신의 지식과 기술을 무료로 공유한다. 나도 유튜브 영상을 보면서 기타를 배웠고, 그것이 큰 도움이 되었다.

둘째, 일상생활에 도움이 되는 유용한 팁을 찾을 수 있다. 요리 레시피, 운동 루틴, 그리고 돈을 절약하는 방법도 배울 수 있다. 예를 들어, 나는 저녁을 만들 때마다 내가 좋아하는 요리 유튜브 채널을 보고, 메뉴를 정한 후, 레시피를 따라 요리한다.

하지만 나는 유튜브에도 몇 가지 단점이 있다고 생각한다. 한때 유튜브를 너무 많이 본 적이 있었는데, 그때는 일할 때 집중하기 어려웠고, 밤에 잠을 자는 데도 영향을 받았다.

또 다른 문제는 유튜브 쇼츠다. 이 짧은 영상은 매우 중독성이 강해서 아무 생각 없이 보면서 시간을 낭비하기 쉽다.

결론적으로, 유튜브는 학습하고 정보를 얻기에 매우 유용한 플랫폼이지만, 중독되지 않도록 주의해야 한다. 유튜브를 현명하게 사용하고 현실 생활과 균형을 맞추려고 노력해야겠다.

유튜브

🗣️ 스피킹1_ 중요 패턴 익히기 [해석]

There was a time when I 동사과거형
: (동사)했던 때가 있었다, 한때 (동사)했었다

- 한때 나는 가수가 되고 싶었지만, 지금은 그냥 취미로 노래한다.

- 한때 나는 술을 너무 많이 마셨지만, 지금은 조금만 마신다.

- 한때 나는 엄격한 다이어트를 했지만, 지금은 건강에 더 집중한다.

🗣️ 스피킹2_ 내 이야기해 봅시다 [해석]

질문 유튜브 자주 보나요?
그렇다면, 가장 좋아하는 유튜브 채널이 뭔가요?

답
- 네, 저는 거의 매일 유튜브를 봅니다. 특히 "빠니보틀" 같은 여행 채널을 좋아해요.

- 네, 저는 유튜브를 많이 봅니다, 특히 밤에 자기 전에요. 제가 가장 좋아하는 채널은 "영국남자"입니다. 정말 웃겨요.

- 그럴 때도 있고, 안 그럴 때도 있어요. 저는 특별히 좋아하는 채널은 없지만, 영화 채널을 보는 것을 즐깁니다.

53강 해외에서 쇼핑하기

👁 본문 눈으로 이해하기

Salesperson : Hello! How can I help you?

Customer : Hi! I'm just looking around.

Salesperson : Alright! Let me know if you need any help.

Customer : Excuse me, do you have this in a smaller size?

Salesperson : Sure! You're holding an extra large. Let me check...
Yes! Here's a large. Would you like to try it on?

Customer : Yes, please. Where is the fitting room?

Salesperson : The fitting rooms are over there. Let me know if
you need a different size.

Customer : I like it! But do you have this in a different color?

Salesperson : Let me check... Yes! We have it in brown and black.

Customer : Can I see the brown one?

Salesperson : Sure! Here you go.

Customer : Great! I'll take this one. Can I pay with my credit
card?

Salesperson : Of course! We accept both cash and credit cards.

Customer : Here you go.

Salesperson : Please insert your card here. Here's your receipt.
Would you like a bag?

Customer : Yes, please. Thank you!

Salesperson : You're welcome! Have a great day!

Customer : Thanks! You too!

👄 본문 소리 내어 읽기

Salesperson : Hello! How can I help you?

Customer : Hi! I'm just looking around.

Salesperson : Alright! Let me know **/** if you need any help.

Customer : Excuse me, **/** do you have this **/** in a smaller size?

Salesperson : Sure! You're holding an extra large. Let me check…
/ Yes! Here's a large. Would you like to try it on?

Customer : Yes, please. Where is the fitting room?

Salesperson : The fitting rooms are over there. Let me know **/** if
you need a different size.

Customer : I like it! But do you have this **/** in a different color?

Salesperson : Let me check… **/** Yes! We have it in brown and black.

Customer : Can I see the brown one?

Salesperson : Sure! Here you go.

Customer : Great! I'll take this one. Can I pay with my credit
card?

Salesperson : Of course! We accept **/** both cash and credit cards.

Customer : Here you go.

Salesperson : Please insert your card here. Here's your receipt.
Would you like a bag?

Customer : Yes, please. Thank you!

Salesperson : You're welcome! Have a great day!

Customer : Thanks! You too!

해외에서 쇼핑하기

👄 **스피킹1_ 중요 패턴 익히기**

Would you like 명사? : (명사) 드릴까요?
Would you like to 동사원형? : (동사) 하실래요?

- Would you like some coffee? Or would you prefer tea?

- Would you like a seat over here, or would you like to
  wait for a different table?

- Would you like anything else? Let me know if you need
  anything!

- Would you like to join us? Or do you have other plans?

👄 **스피킹2_ 내 이야기해 봅시다**

옷 쇼핑할 때 유용한 표현들

A
- I'm looking for this jacket. Do you have this in your store?

- Is this on sale? How much is it after the discount?

- Do you accept exchanges and returns?
  → Yes, we accept exchanges and returns within 30 days with the original receipt.
  → Sorry, we do not accept exchanges or returns on sale items.

- Thank you, but I think I'll pass on this one.

👁 본문 [해석]

판매 직원 : 안녕하세요! 어떻게 도와드릴까요?

손님 : 안녕하세요! 그냥 둘러보고 있어요.

판매 직원 : 알겠습니다! 도움이 필요하시면 알려주세요.

손님 : 실례하지만, 이거 더 작은 사이즈 있나요?

판매 직원 : 물론이죠! 지금 들고 계신 건 엑스트라 라지예요. 확인해볼게요... 네! 여기 라지 사이즈 있습니다. 한 번 입어 보시겠어요?

손님 : 네, 부탁드려요. 탈의실은 어디에 있나요?

판매 직원 : 저쪽에 탈의실이 있어요. 다른 사이즈가 필요하시면 말씀해 주세요.

손님 : 마음에 들어요! 그런데 이거 다른 색상도 있나요?

판매 직원 : 확인해볼게요... 네! 갈색과 검은색이 있습니다.

손님 : 갈색 색상 좀 볼 수 있을까요?

판매 직원 : 물론이죠! 여기 있습니다.

손님 : 좋아요! 이걸로 할게요. 신용카드로 결제할 수 있나요?

판매 직원 : 물론이죠! 현금과 신용카드 둘 다 가능합니다.

손님 : 여기요.

판매 직원 : 카드를 여기에 삽입해 주세요. 여기 영수증입니다. 봉투 필요하세요?

손님 : 네, 부탁드려요. 감사합니다!

판매 직원 : 아닙니다! 좋은 하루 보내세요!

손님 : 감사합니다! 좋은 하루 되세요!

53강 해외에서 쇼핑하기

🗣 스피킹1_ 중요 패턴 익히기 [해석]

Would you like 명사? : (명사) 드릴까요?
Would you like to 동사원형? : (동사) 하실래요?

- 커피 드실래요? 아니면 차가 더 좋으신가요?

- 여기 앉으시겠어요, 아니면 다른 테이블이 날 때까지 기다리시겠어요?

- 다른 거 더 필요하세요? 필요하신 거 있으면 말씀해 주세요!

- 우리랑 함께 하실래요? 아니면 다른 계획이 있으세요?

🗣 스피킹2_ 내 이야기해 봅시다 [해석]

옷 쇼핑할 때 유용한 표현들

- 이 재킷을 찾고 있어요. 이거 이 매장에 있나요?

- 이거 세일 중인가요? 할인 후 가격이 얼마인가요?

- 교환 및 환불이 가능하나요?

  ➔ 네, 영수증이 있으면 30일 이내 교환 및 반품이 가능합니다.

  ➔ 죄송합니다. 세일 상품은 교환 및 반품이 불가능합니다.

- 감사합니다만, 이번에는 그냥 넘어갈게요. (안 살게요)

54강 공연 안내방송

👁 **본문 눈으로 이해하기**

<Pre-show Announcement>

Ladies and gentlemen, welcome to the Minskoff Theatre. Tonight's performance of The Lion King will begin shortly. At this time, please turn off or silence all cell phones and electronic devices. Photography and video recording are strictly prohibited. Please note that outside food and beverages are not permitted inside the theater. The show will begin in just a few moments. Please take your seats and enjoy the performance!

<Intermission Announcement>

Ladies and gentlemen, Act 1 of the Lion King has now concluded. We will have a 15-minute intermission. Please feel free to visit the lobby for refreshments, restrooms, and merchandise. We kindly ask that you return to your seats promptly before the second act begins. When re-entering the theater, please have your tickets ready. Thank you and enjoy the rest of the show.

<Post-Show Announcement>

Ladies and gentlemen, thank you for joining us for tonight's performance of The Lion King. We hope you enjoyed the show! As you exit, please take all personal belongings with you. On behalf of the cast and crew, we appreciate your support and hope to see you again. Have a wonderful evening!

👄 본문 소리 내어 읽기

<Pre-show Announcement>

Ladies and gentlemen, / welcome to the Minskoff Theatre.
Tonight's performance of The Lion King / will begin shortly. At this
time, / please turn off or silence / all cell phones and electronic
devices. Photography and video recording / are strictly prohibited.
Please note that / outside food and beverages / are not
permitted / inside the theater. The show will begin / in just a few
moments. Please take your seats / and enjoy the performance!

<Intermission Announcement>

Ladies and gentlemen, / Act 1 of the Lion King has now concluded.
We will have a 15-minute intermission. Please feel free to visit the
lobby / for refreshments, restrooms, and merchandise. We kindly
ask that / you return to your seats promptly / before the second
act begins. When re-entering the theater, / please have your
tickets ready. Thank you and enjoy the rest of the show.

<Post-Show Announcement>

Ladies and gentlemen, / thank you for joining us / for tonight's
performance of The Lion King. We hope you enjoyed the show! As
you exit, / please take all personal belongings with you. On behalf
of the cast and crew, / we appreciate your support / and hope to
see you again. Have a wonderful evening!

👄 **스피킹1_ 중요 패턴 익히기**

Please feel free to 동사원형 : 편히 (동사)해 주세요

- Please feel free to have some snacks. There's plenty, so help yourself!

- Please feel free to contact me anytime. I'm happy to help.

- Please feel free to look around. Take your time and enjoy!

 **54강** 공연 안내방송

👄 **스피킹2_ 내 이야기해 봅시다**

Q Have you seen any shows recently?

A ▪ Yes, I saw a play last month. It was better than I expected.

▪ Not recently, but I went to a BlackPink concert two years ago. It was fantastic!

▪ No, I haven't. But if I get the chance, I'd love to go to a BTS concert.

공연 안내방송

👁 본문 [해석]

<공연 전 안내방송>

신사숙녀 여러분, 민스코프 극장에 오신 것을 환영합니다. 오늘 밤 라이온 킹 공연이 곧 시작됩니다. 지금 이 순간, 모든 휴대전화 및 전자기기의 전원을 끄거나 무음 모드로 설정해 주시기 바랍니다. 사진 촬영 및 동영상 녹화는 엄격히 금지되어 있습니다.외부 음식 및 음료 반입은 허용되지 않으니 유의해 주세요. 공연이 곧 시작되오니 자리에 착석해 주시고, 공연을 즐겨 주시기 바랍니다!

<인터미션 안내방송>

신사숙녀 여러분, 라이온 킹 1막이 종료되었습니다. 이제부터 15분간의 인터미션이 진행됩니다. 로비에서 다과, 화장실, 기념품 구매를 이용하실 수 있습니다. 2막이 시작되기 전에 제시간에 좌석으로 돌아와 주시길 부탁드립니다. 재입장 시에는 티켓을 준비해 주세요. 감사합니다. 남은 공연도 즐겨 주시기 바랍니다!

<공연 후 안내방송>

신사숙녀 여러분, 오늘 라이온 킹 공연에 함께해 주셔서 감사합니다. 즐거운 시간 되셨기를 바랍니다! 퇴장하실 때는 모든 개인 소지품을 잊지 말고 챙겨 주시기 바랍니다. 출연진과 제작진을 대표하여 여러분의 성원에 감사드리며, 다시 만나 뵙기를 기대하겠습니다.

즐거운 저녁 보내세요!

👄 스피킹1_ 중요 패턴 익히기 [해석]

Please feel free to 동사원형 : 편히 (동사)해 주세요

- 간식 편하게 드세요. 많이 있으니 마음껏 드세요.

- 언제든 편하게 연락하세요. 기꺼이 도와드릴게요.

- 편하게 둘러보세요. 천천히 구경하면서 즐기세요!

👄 스피킹2_ 내 이야기해 봅시다 [해석]

질문 최근에 공연 본 적 있나요?

답
- 네, 지난달에 연극을 봤어요. 예상보다 더 좋았어요.

- 최근에는 아니지만, 2년 전에 블랙핑크 콘서트에 갔었어요. 정말 환상적이었어요!

- 아니요, 못 봤어요. 하지만 기회가 되면 BTS 콘서트에 꼭 가보고 싶어요.

 **55강**  해외에서 약 사기

◉ 본문 눈으로 이해하기

Pharmacist : Hello, how can I help you?

Customer : Hi, my son suddenly got a rash on his arms and legs. He had shrimp pasta for lunch.

Pharmacist : Has he eaten shrimp before?

Customer : Yes, he has, and he was fine before. But this time, he got a rash.

Pharmacist : He might be developing an allergy. Does he have any other symptoms, like trouble breathing or swelling?

Customer : No, just the rash.

Pharmacist : How old is he?

Customer : He's seven.

Pharmacist : You can give him Children's Benadryl. It should help with the itching.

Customer : Could you help me find it?

Pharmacist : Of course! Follow me. Here it is.

Customer : How much should I give him?

Pharmacist : Give him one teaspoon every six hours, if needed.

Customer : Thank you!

Pharmacist : You're welcome. If his symptoms get worse, take him to a doctor immediately.

Customer : Got it! Thanks a lot!

55강 해외에서 약 사기

👄 본문 소리 내어 읽기

Pharmacist : Hello, how can I help you?

Customer : Hi, my son suddenly got a rash / on his arms and legs. He had shrimp pasta for lunch.

Pharmacist : Has he eaten shrimp before?

Customer : Yes, he has, / and he was fine before. But this time, / he got a rash.

Pharmacist : He might be developing an allergy. Does he have any other symptoms, / like trouble breathing or swelling?

Customer : No, just the rash.

Pharmacist : How old is he?

Customer : He's seven.

Pharmacist : You can give him / Children's Benadryl. It should help / with the itching.

Customer : Could you help me find it?

Pharmacist : Of course! Follow me. Here it is.

Customer : How much should I give him?

Pharmacist : Give him one teaspoon every six hours, / if needed.

Customer : Thank you!

Pharmacist : You're welcome. If his symptoms get worse, / take him to a doctor immediately.

Customer : Got it! Thanks a lot!

55강 해외에서 약 사기

give A(누구) + B(무언가) : A에게 B를 주다

- I'll give you a ride to the airport. Let me know when you're ready.

- It was his birthday yesterday. Did you give him a birthday present?

- I'm in the middle of something. Can you give me some time?

- I waved at her. She gave me a smile.

👄 **스피킹2_ 내 이야기해 봅시다**

A : Hello, how can I help you?
B : I have a sore throat.
A : How long have you had it?
B : It started yesterday.

✅ **증상명**

No	Symptoms (증상)	English
1	fever (고열)	I have a fever.
2	chills and body aches (오한과 몸살)	I have chills and body aches.
3	sore throat (목아픔)	I have a sore throat.
4	runny nose and congestion (콧물과 코막힘)	I have a runny nose and congestion.
5	cough (기침)	I have a cough.
6	stomachache (복통)	I have a stomachache.
7	indigestion (소화불량/체함)	I have indigestion.
8	nauseous (울렁거리는)	I feel nauseous.
9	throw up (구토하다)	I threw up.
10	diarrhea (설사)	I have diarrhea.
11	sprain (삐끗하다)	I sprained my ankle.
12	itchy and irritated (가렵고 따가운)	My eyes are itchy and irritated.
13	cut (베임)	I have a cut on my finger.
14	burn(화상)	I have a burn on my finger.
15	sunburn (햇볕에 데임)	I have a sunburn on my shoulder.
16	be bitten by (~에 물리다)	I was bitten by an insect.

55강 해외에서 약 사기

👁 본문 [해석]

약사 : 안녕하세요, 어떻게 도와드릴까요?

손님 : 안녕하세요, 제 아들이 갑자기 팔과 다리에 발진이 났어요. 점심으로 새우 파스타를 먹었어요.

약사 : 이전에도 새우를 먹어 본 적이 있나요?

손님 : 네, 먹어 봤고 그때는 괜찮았어요. 그런데 이번에는 발진이 났어요.

약사 : 알레르기가 생기는 것일 수도 있어요. 숨 쉬기 어렵거나 부어오르는 등의 다른 증상이 있나요?

손님 : 아니요, 발진만 있어요.

약사 : 아이가 몇 살인가요?

손님 : 일곱 살이에요.

약사 : 어린이용 베나드릴을 먹이면 돼요. 가려움증을 완화하는 데 도움이 될 거예요.

손님 : 어디 있는지 찾아주실 수 있나요?

약사 : 물론이죠! 따라오세요. 여기 있어요.

손님 : 얼마나 먹여야 하나요?

약사 : 필요하면 6시간마다 한 티스푼씩 주세요.

손님 : 감사합니다!

약사 : 별말씀을요. 만약 증상이 더 심해지면 바로 병원에 데려가세요.

손님 : 알겠습니다! 정말 감사합니다!

⬎ 스피킹1_ 중요 패턴 익히기 [해석]

give A(누구) + B(무언가) : A에게 B를 주다

- 공항까지 태워다 줄게. 준비되면 알려줘.

- 어제가 그의 생일이었어. 생일 선물 줬어?

- 나 지금 뭔가 하고 있어. 시간 좀 줄 수 있어?

- 내가 그녀에게 손을 흔들었어. 그녀가 미소를 지어 줬어.

55강 해외에서 약 사기

🗣 **스피킹2_ 내 이야기해 봅시다 [해석]**

A : 안녕하세요, 어떻게 도와드릴까요?

B : 목이 아파서요.

A : 얼마나 오래 그 증상이 있었나요?

B : 어제 시작됐어요.

⊘ 증상명

No	Symptoms (증상)	English
1	fever (고열)	열이 있어요.
2	chills and body aches (오한과 몸살)	오한과 몸살이 있어요.
3	sore throat (목아픔)	목이 아파요.
4	runny nose and congestion (콧물과 코막힘)	콧물과 코막힘이 있어요.
5	cough (기침)	기침이 나요
6	stomachache (복통)	배가 아파요.
7	indigestion (소화불량/체함)	체했어요.
8	nauseous (울렁거리는)	속이 울렁거려요.
9	throw up (구토하다)	토했어요.
10	diarrhea (설사)	설사해요.
11	sprain (삐끗하다)	발목을 삐었어요.
12	itchy and irritated (가렵고 따가운)	눈이 가렵고 따가와요.
13	cut (베임)	손가락 베었어요.
14	burn(화상)	손가락에 화상 입었어요.
15	sunburn (햇볕에 데임)	햇볕에 데였어요.
16	be bitten by (~에 물리다)	벌레 물렸어요.

MEMO

56강 나의 인생책

👁 **본문 눈으로 이해하기**

<My All-Time Favorite Book>

My all-time favorite book is Mu-soyu by Beopjeong Sunim. Although I am not a Buddhist, I really related to that book. In Mu-soyu, the author talks about living simply and letting go of material things. I was touched by his way of looking at life and how he finds happiness in inner peace.

Reading this book changed my view on what is important. I learned that true happiness does not come from having many things, but from being content with what I have. The book taught me to value love, kindness, and peace over material possessions. I try to apply these ideas in my daily life.

Even though I do not follow Buddhism, Mu-soyu has greatly influenced my life philosophy. As the book suggests, I am currently living my daily life as minimally and simply as possible. I also want to live a life that focuses on values rather than possessions.

👄 **본문 소리 내어 읽기**

<My All-Time Favorite Book>

My all-time favorite book is Mu-soyu / by Beopjeong Sunim.
Although I am not a Buddhist, / I really related to that book.
In Mu-soyu, / the author talks about living simply / and
letting go of material things. I was touched / by his way of
looking at life / and how he finds happiness / in inner peace.
Reading this book / changed my view / on what is important.
I learned that / true happiness / does not come from having
many things, / but from being content / with what I have. The
book taught me / to value love, kindness, and peace / over
material possessions. I try to apply these ideas / in my daily
life.

Even though I do not follow Buddhism, / Mu-soyu has greatly
influenced my life philosophy. As the book suggests, / I am
currently living my daily life / as minimally and simply as
possible. I also want to live a life / that focuses on values /
rather than possessions.

🗣 스피킹1_ 중요 패턴 익히기

I'm currently 동사ing : 나는 현재 (동사)하는 중이다

- I'm currently living in London. I moved here for work, and I'm pretty happy with my life here.

- I'm currently working on a new project. It's quite challenging, so I'm struggling a bit.

- I'm currently taking tennis lessons, and I feel like I'm improving.

 **56강** 나의 인생책

👄 **스피킹2_ 내 이야기해 봅시다**

Q What's your all-time favorite book?

A ▪ My all-time favorite book is Demian. I really relate to the main character, and the story is so moving.

▪ I love Romance of the Three Kingdoms. It's full of strategy, leadership, and amazing characters. Every time I read it, I pick up something new.

▪ I'd say Tuesdays with Morrie. It gives deep insights into life and death. I highly recommend it.

나의 인생책

👁 본문 [해석]

<나의 인생책>

내 인생 책은 법정 스님의 『무소유』입니다. 비록 내가 불교 신자는 아니지만, 이 책의 사상에 정말 공감합니다. 『무소유』에서 저자는 단순하게 살아가며 물질적인 것들을 내려놓는 것에 대해 이야기합니다. 나는 그가 인생을 바라보는 방식과 내면의 평화 속에서 행복을 찾는 모습에 감동받았습니다.

이 책을 읽으면서 무엇이 중요한지에 대한 내 관점이 바뀌었습니다. 나는 진정한 행복은 많은 것을 소유하는 데서 오는 것이 아니라, 내가 가진 것에 만족하는 데서 온다는 것을 배웠습니다. 이 책은 물질적 소유물보다 사랑, 친절, 평화를 소중히 여기는 법을 가르쳐 주었습니다. 나는 이러한 생각들을 일상생활에 적용하려고 노력합니다.

비록 나는 불교를 따르지는 않지만, 『무소유』는 내 인생 철학에 큰 영향을 주었습니다. 책에서 제안하는 대로, 나는 현재 가능한 한 최소한으로 단순하게 일상을 살아가고 있습니다. 또한, 나는 소유물보다는 가치에 집중하는 삶을 살고 싶습니다.

나의 인생책

👄 스피킹1_ 중요 패턴 익히기 [해석]

I'm currently 동사ing : 나는 현재 (동사)하는 중이다

- 나는 현재 런던에 사는 중이다. 일 때문에 여기로 이사 왔고, 여기 내 삶에 꽤 만족한다.

- 나는 현재 새 프로젝트에 대해 일하는 중이다. 꽤 힘들어서, 조금 고전하는 중이다.

- 나는 현재 테니스 레슨을 받고 있는데, 실력이 느는 것 같다.

👄 스피킹2 내 이야기해 봅시다 [해석]

질문 당신의 인생책은 무엇인가요?

답
- 내가 가장 좋아하는 책은 『데미안』이야. 나는 주인공에게 정말 공감하고, 이야기가 정말 감동적이야.

- 나는 『삼국지』를 정말 좋아해. 전략, 리더십, 그리고 놀라운 캐릭터들로 가득 차 있어. 읽을 때마다 새로운 걸 배우게 돼.

- 『나라면 모리와 함께한 화요일』을 꼽을 것 같아. 삶과 죽음에 대한 깊은 통찰을 제공해 줘. 나는 이 책을 강력히 추천해.

57강 인생영화

👁 **본문 눈으로 이해하기**

Alice : Hey Jinsu, do you have a favorite movie?

Jinsu : Oh, that's an easy question! I love sci-fi and fantasy movies, and my all-time favorite is The Lord of the Rings.

Alice : Oh, that's a great movie! Do you watch it often?

Jinsu : Yeah, I never get tired of it. I watch it whenever I have time. What about you? What's your favorite movie?

Alice : My all-time favorite movie is Forrest Gump. Have you seen it?

Jinsu : Actually, no, I haven't. But I've heard it's really good.

Alice : Oh, you should definitely watch it!

Jinsu : Yeah? Who's in it again? I don't really remember.

Alice : Tom Hanks plays the main character, Forrest Gump. He's amazing in this movie!

Jinsu : Oh, right! Now I remember. What's it about?

Alice : It's a really touching story about one man's life. But it's also fun because it shows a lot of American history in an interesting way.

Jinsu : That sounds great. Maybe I should watch it soon.

Alice : Yeah, you should! I think you'll like it.

57강 인생영화

👄 본문 소리 내어 읽기

Alice : Hey Jinsu, do you have a favorite movie?

Jinsu : Oh, that's an easy question! I love sci-fi and fantasy movies, **/** and my all-time favorite **/** is The Lord of the Rings.

Alice : Oh, that's a great movie! Do you watch it often?

Jinsu : Yeah, I never get tired of it. I watch it **/** whenever I have time. What about you? What's your favorite movie?

Alice : My all-time favorite movie **/** is Forrest Gump. Have you seen it?

Jinsu : Actually, no, I haven't. But I've heard **/** it's really good.

Alice : Oh, you should definitely watch it!

Jinsu : Yeah? Who's in it again? I don't really remember.

Alice : Tom Hanks plays the main character, Forrest Gump. He's amazing in this movie!

Jinsu : Oh, right! Now I remember. What's it about?

Alice : It's a really touching story **/** about one man's life. But it's also fun **/** because it shows a lot of American history **/** in an interesting way.

Jinsu : That sounds great. Maybe I should watch it soon.

Alice : Yeah, you should! I think you'll like it.

🫦 스피킹1_ 중요 패턴 익히기

get tired of 명사/동명사 : ~에 질리다

- I'm getting tired of eating pizza these days. I need a break from greasy food.

- I never get tired of Gomtang. It's my perfect comfort food.

- She got tired of his lies, and broke up with him.

- Are you getting tired of your routine? Try something new!

57강 인생영화

👄 스피킹2_ 내 이야기해 봅시다

Q What's your all-time favorite movie?

A
- My all-time favorite movie is Casablanca. It's an old movie, but I love the atmosphere of the movie.

- I really like Parasite. It was so intense and thought-provoking.

- I love About Time. It's such a heartwarming and touching story.

👁 **본문 [해석]**

Alice : 진수, 네가 제일 좋아하는 영화 있어?

Jinsu : 오, 그건 쉬운 질문이네! 나는 SF랑 판타지 영화를 정말 좋아하는
데, 내가 제일 좋아하는 영화는 『반지의 제왕』이야.

Alice : 오, 그거 정말 좋은 영화지! 자주 봐?

Jinsu : 응, 질리지 않아. 시간 날 때마다 봐. 너는 어때? 너가 가장 좋아
하는 영화는 뭐야?

Alice : 내가 가장 좋아하는 영화는 『포레스트 검프』야. 본 적 있어?

Jinsu : 사실, 아니. 아직 못 봤어. 근데 정말 좋은 영화라고 들었어.

Alice : 오, 꼭 봐야 해!

Jinsu : 그래? 누가 나오는 영화지? 잘 기억이 안 나.

Alice : 톰 행크스가 주인공 포레스트 검프 역할을 해. 이 영화에서 정말
멋진 연기를 했어!

Jinsu : 아, 맞다! 이제 기억나. 어떤 내용이야?

Alice : 한 남자의 인생을 감동적으로 그린 이야기야. 그런데 미국 역사
를 많이 담고 있어서 재미있기도 해.

Jinsu : 재미있겠다. 조만간 한 번 봐야겠네.

Alice : 응, 꼭 봐! 너도 좋아할 거야.

인생영화

👄 **스피킹1_ 중요 패턴 익히기 [해석]**

get tired of 명사/동명사 : ~에 질리다

- 요즘 피자가 질려. 기름진 음식에서 좀 벗어나야겠어.

- 나는 곰탕이 절대 질리지 않아. 내게 딱 맞는 위로 음식이야.

- 그녀는 그의 거짓말에 질려서 헤어졌어.

- 일상이 지겨워? 새로운 걸 시도해 봐!

👄 **스피킹2_ 내 이야기해 봅시다 [해석]**

질문 당신의 인생영화는 무엇인가요?

답
- 내가 가장 좋아하는 영화는 『카사블랑카』야. 오래된 영화지만, 나는 그 영화의 분위기를 정말 좋아해.

- 나는 『기생충』을 정말 좋아해. 정말 강렬하고 많은 생각을 하게 만드는 영화였어.

- 나는 『어바웃 타임』을 사랑해. 정말 따뜻하고 감동적인 이야기야.

 **58강** **작은 습관의 힘**

◉ **본문 눈으로 이해하기**

<Small Habits Can Change Your Life>

Many people want to change their lives. They want to be healthier, happier, or more successful. Instead of focusing on big goals, starting with small habits is a more effective approach.

If you start with a small habit, it is easy to maintain. For example, if you want to exercise more, you don't need to run for an hour. You can start with five minutes of stretching. If you want to learn a new language, you don't have to study for three hours a day. You can start by practicing for 10 minutes or memorizing one useful sentence each day. If you want to read more, you don't have to finish a book in one day. You can read one page every night.

Small habits become bigger over time. If you do them every day, they will grow. After a few weeks or months, you will see big changes in your life. Don't wait for the perfect moment. Start with a small habit today!

 **58강** 작은 습관의 힘

👄 **본문 소리 내어 읽기**

<Small Habits Can Change Your Life>

Many people want to change their lives. They want to be healthier, / happier, / or more successful. Instead of focusing on big goals, / starting with small habits / is a more effective approach.

If you start with a small habit, / it is easy to maintain. For example, / if you want to exercise more, / you don't need to run / for an hour. You can start / with five minutes of stretching. If you want to learn a new language, / you don't have to study / for three hours a day. You can start / by practicing for 10 minutes / or memorizing one useful sentence each day. If you want to read more, / you don't have to finish a book / in one day. You can read one page every night.

Small habits become bigger / over time. If you do them every day, / they will grow. After a few weeks or months, / you will see big changes / in your life. Don't wait for the perfect moment. Start with a small habit today!

58강 작은 습관의 힘

👄 스피킹1_ 중요 패턴 익히기

You don't have to 동사원형 : (동사) 하지 않아도 된다

- You don't have to worry about it. I'll take care of it.

- You don't have to hurry. We have plenty of time.

- You don't have to bring anything. Just bring yourself.

- You don't have to dress formally. Just come as you are.
  It's a casual dinner.

🫦 스피킹2_ 내 이야기해 봅시다

Q Do you have any daily habits?

A
- Yes, I do. I always start my day with a glass of lukewarm water. After that, I usually do some light stretching.

- Yes, I read before bed every night. After that, I set my alarm for the next day.

- Yes, I walk my dog after dinner every day. We take a walk in the park near my place.

- Yes, I write in my journal every day, and reflect on my day.

58강 작은 습관의 힘

◉ 본문 [해석]

<작은 습관이 인생을 바꿀 수 있다>

많은 사람들은 자신의 삶을 변화시키고 싶어 합니다. 그들은 더 건강하고, 더 행복하고, 더 성공적인 삶을 원합니다. 하지만 큰 목표에 집중하는 대신, 작은 습관부터 시작하는 것이 더 효과적인 방법입니다.

작은 습관부터 시작하면 쉽게 유지할 수 있습니다. 예를 들어, 운동을 더 하고 싶다면 한 시간 동안 뛸 필요가 없습니다. 5분간 스트레칭부터 시작할 수 있습니다. 새로운 언어를 배우고 싶다면 하루에 3시간씩 공부할 필요가 없습니다. 대신 매일 10분 동안 연습하거나 유용한 문장을 하나씩 외울 수 있습니다. 독서를 더 하고 싶다면 하루 만에 책 한 권을 다 읽을 필요가 없습니다. 매일 밤 한 페이지씩 읽으면 됩니다.

작은 습관들은 시간이 지나면서 점점 커집니다. 매일 지속하면 그것들은 성장할 것입니다. 몇 주 또는 몇 달 후에는 당신의 삶에서 큰 변화를 보게 될 것입니다. 완벽한 순간을 기다리지 마세요. 오늘부터 작은 습관을 시작하세요!

58강 작은 습관의 힘

👄 스피킹1_ 중요 패턴 익히기 [해석]

You don't have to 동사원형 : (동사) 하지 않아도 된다

- 그거 걱정할 필요 없어. 내가 알아서 할게.

- 서두를 필요 없어. 우리 시간 충분해.

- 아무것도 가져올 필요 없어. 그냥 몸만 오면 돼.

- 정장 입을 필요 없어. 그냥 편하게 와. 편한 저녁 식사 자리야.

👄 스피킹2_ 내 이야기해 봅시다 [해석]

질문 당신은 매일 하는 습관이 있나요?

답
- 네, 맞아요. 저는 항상 미지근한 물 한 잔으로 하루를 시작해요. 그 다음에는 보통 가벼운 스트레칭을 해요.

- 네, 저는 매일 밤 자기 전에 책을 읽어요. 그 다음에는 다음 날을 위해 알람을 맞춰요.

- 네, 저는 매일 저녁 식사 후에 강아지를 산책시켜요. 집 근처 공원에서 산책을 해요.

- 네, 저는 매일 일기를 쓰면서 제 하루를 돌아봐요.

 **59강**

컴플레인 하기

◉ 본문 눈으로 이해하기

Guest : Excuse me, I have a problem with my room.

Front Desk Agent : Oh, I'm sorry to hear that. What seems to be the problem?

Guest : Well, the room is not very clean. I found some hair on the bed, and the cups have dust on them.

Front Desk Agent : Oh, I sincerely apologize for that. That shouldn't happen.

Guest : Also, the water pressure in the bathroom is too low. The shower is very weak.

Front Desk Agent : I see. I'm really sorry for the inconvenience. I can send housekeeping to clean the room and have maintenance check the water pressure.

Guest : Actually, would it be possible to change rooms?

Front Desk Agent : Of course. Let me check the availability.

(after checking)

We do have another room available. Would you like a similar room on a different floor?

Guest : Yes, that would be great.

Front Desk Agent : Alright. I'll arrange the room change right away. Here is your new room key.

Guest : Thank you so much. I really appreciate your help.

Front Desk Agent : You're very welcome! Please let us know if you need anything else.

59강 컴플레인 하기

👄 본문 소리 내어 읽기

Guest : Excuse me, **/** I have a problem with my room.

Front Desk Agent : Oh, I'm sorry to hear that. What seems to be the problem?

Guest : Well, the room is not very clean. I found some hair on the bed, **/** and the cups have dust on them.

Front Desk Agent : Oh, I sincerely apologize for that. That shouldn't happen.

Guest : Also, **/** the water pressure in the bathroom **/** is too low. The shower is very weak.

Front Desk Agent : I see. I'm really sorry **/** for the inconvenience. I can send housekeeping **/** to clean the room **/** and have maintenance check the water pressure.

Guest : Actually, **/** would it be possible to change rooms?

Front Desk Agent : Of course. Let me check the availability.

(after checking)
We do have another room available. Would you like a similar room **/** on a different floor?

Guest : Yes, that would be great.

Front Desk Agent : Alright. I'll arrange the room change right away. Here is your new room key.

Guest : Thank you so much. I really appreciate your help.

Front Desk Agent : You're very welcome! Please let us know **/** if you need anything else.

👄 **스피킹1_ 중요 패턴 익히기**

Would it be possible to 동사원형? : (동사)하는 게 가능할까요?

- Would it be possible to get a refund? The item is defective.

- Would it be possible to check my luggage again? It hasn't arrived yet.

- Would it be possible to get a new dish? I found a hair in my food.

59강 컴플레인 하기

👄 **스피킹2_ 내 이야기해 봅시다**

A : Hello, how may I help you?

B : Hi, I have a problem. My room is too cold. Could you check the heating, please?

A
- My room is too hot. Could you check the air conditioning, please?

- The TV isn't working. Could you check it, please?

- There's no hot water. Could you fix it, please?

- My room is very noisy. Would it be possible to change rooms?

- The Wi-Fi isn't working. It keeps disconnecting.

59강 컴플레인 하기

◎ 본문 [해석]

손님 : 실례합니다. 제 방에 문제가 있어요.

호텔 직원 : 아, 죄송합니다. 어떤 문제가 있으신가요?

손님 : 음, 방이 별로 깨끗하지 않아요. 침대에서 머리카락을 발견했고, 컵에는 먼지가 있어요.

호텔 직원 : 아, 정말 죄송합니다. 그런 일이 있어서는 안 되는데요.

손님 : 그리고 욕실의 수압이 너무 낮아요. 샤워기가 약하게 나와요.

호텔 직원 : 그렇군요. 불편을 끼쳐드려 정말 죄송합니다. 제가 청소 담당을 보내서 방을 청소하도록 하고, 유지 보수 담당이 수압을 확인하도록 하겠습니다.

손님 : 사실, 방을 바꿀 수 있을까요?

호텔 직원 : 물론이죠. 가능 여부(빈 방이 있는지) 확인해 보겠습니다. (확인 후) 빈 객실이 하나 있습니다. 비슷한 타입의 방을 다른 층으로 변경해 드릴까요?

손님 : 네, 그렇게 해 주시면 좋겠어요.

호텔 직원 : 알겠습니다. 바로 방 변경을 도와드릴게요. 여기 새 객실 키입니다.

손님 : 정말 감사합니다. 도움에 진심으로 감사해요.

호텔 직원 : 천만에요! 다른 필요한 것이 있으면 언제든 말씀해 주세요.

59강 컴플레인 하기

🗣 스피킹1_ 중요 패턴 익히기 [해석]

Would it be possible to 동사원형? : (동사)하는 게 가능할까요?

- 환불을 받을 수 있을까요? 제품에 결함이 있습니다.

- 제 짐을 다시 확인해 주실 수 있을까요? 아직 도착하지 않았어요.

- 새 요리를 받을 수 있을까요? 음식에서 머리카락을 발견했어요.

🗣 스피킹2_ 내 이야기해 봅시다 [해석]

A : 안녕하세요, 어떻게 도와드릴까요?
B : 안녕하세요, 문제가 있어요. 제 방이 너무 추워요. 난방 좀 확인해 주
시겠어요?

답
- 제 방이 너무 더워요. 에어컨을 확인해 주실 수 있을까요?

- TV가 작동하지 않아요. 확인해 주실 수 있을까요?

- 뜨거운 물이 안 나와요. 고쳐 주실 수 있을까요?

- 제 방이 너무 시끄러운데, 방을 바꿀 수 있을까요?

- 와이파이가 작동하지 않아요. 계속 끊겨요.

60강 나의 영어 여정

👁 **본문 눈으로 이해하기**

<Three Months, One Big Achievement: My English Journey>

When I turned 50, I decided to study English again. At first, I wasn't sure how to start. But then, I found a YouTube channel called Guide English. That was the moment my English journey truly began.

The class I joined was BomBom Class, a three-month online English course. From Monday to Friday, I watched a lesson for about 30 minutes. After the lesson, I recorded myself reading the day's text aloud. Then, I uploaded my recording to a group chat as my daily homework.

Sometimes, I wanted to give up. In my busy daily life, studying English every day was a big challenge. But when I saw other classmates doing their homework, I felt motivated to continue. Day by day, lesson by lesson, I kept moving forward.

Now, after three months of hard work, I finally finished this big challenge. I feel very proud and happy. It wasn't always easy, but I proved to myself that I can do it.

My next goal is to travel freely, not with a tour group, but on my own. I want to speak English with people from other countries and experience the world in a new way. My English journey doesn't end here—it's just beginning!

👄 **본문 소리 내어 읽기**

<Three Months, One Big Achievement: My English Journey>

When I turned 50, / I decided to study English again. At first, / I wasn't sure how to start. But then, I found a YouTube channel / called Guide English. That was the moment / my English journey truly began.

The class I joined / was BomBom Class, / a three-month online English course. From Monday to Friday, / I watched a lesson / for about 30 minutes. After the lesson, / I recorded myself / reading the day's text aloud. Then, / I uploaded my recording / to a group chat / as my daily homework.

Sometimes, / I wanted to give up. In my busy daily life, / studying English every day / was a big challenge. But when I saw other classmates doing their homework, / I felt motivated to continue. Day by day, / lesson by lesson, / I kept moving forward.

Now, / after three months of hard work, / I finally finished this big challenge. I feel very proud and happy. It wasn't always easy, / but I proved to myself / that I can do it.

My next goal is to travel freely, / not with a tour group, / but on my own. I want to speak English / with people from other countries / and experience the world / in a new way. My English journey doesn't end here—/ it's just beginning!

60강 나의 영어 여정

👄 스피킹1_ 중요 패턴 익히기

That was the moment 주어 + 동사

: 그게 (주어)가 (동사)한 순간이었다 = 그 순간 (주어)가 (동사)했다

- That was the moment I decided to quit my job. I knew I needed a change in my life.

- That was the moment I felt truly happy. I had nothing to envy.

- That was the moment I realized I was late. I started running as fast as I could.

👄 **스피킹2_ 내 이야기해 봅시다**

Q **What would you like to do once your English gets better?**

A ▪ I'd like to travel abroad, and talk to locals in English.

▪ I want to read English books, and watch TED talks without subtitles.

▪ I want to search for information in English on Google.

▪ I want to understand and enjoy English YouTube channels.

60강 나의 영어 여정

👁 **본문 [해석]**

<세 달, 하나의 큰 성취: 나의 영어 여정>

내가 50세가 되었을 때, 다시 영어 공부를 하기로 결심했다. 처음에는 어떻게 시작해야 할지 몰랐다. 그러던 중, <길잡이 영어>라는 유튜브 채널을 발견하게 되었다. 그 순간이 바로 나의 영어 여정이 본격적으로 시작된 순간이었다.

내가 참여한 수업은 BomBom Class라는 3개월 과정의 온라인 영어 강의였다. 월요일부터 금요일까지 하루 약 30분 동안 강의를 들었다. 강의를 들은 후에는 그날의 본문을 소리 내어 읽고 녹음했다. 그리고 그 녹음을 단톡방에 올리는 것이 매일의 숙제였다.

때때로 포기하고 싶을 때도 있었다. 바쁜 일상 속에서 매일 영어를 공부하는 것은 큰 도전이었다. 하지만 단톡방에서 다른 동급생들이 숙제를 하는 모습을 보면서 나도 계속해야겠다는 자극을 받았다. 하루하루, 한 강 한 강, 꾸준히 나아갔다.

그리고 마침내, 3개월간의 노력 끝에 이 큰 도전을 완수했다. 나는 매우 뿌듯하고 행복하다. 쉽지 않은 과정이었지만, 결국 해낼 수 있다는 것을 스스로에게 증명해 보였다.

나의 다음 목표는 패키지여행이 아닌, 자유롭게 여행하는 것이다. 외국인들과 직접 영어로 대화하며 새로운 방식으로 세상을 경험해 보고 싶다. 나의 영어 여정은 여기서 끝이 아니다—이제 다시 시작이다!

60강 나의 영어 여정

🫦 스피킹1_ 중요 패턴 익히기 [해석]

That was the moment 주어 + 동사
: 그게 (주어)가 (동사)한 순간이었다 = 그 순간 (주어)가 (동사)했다

- 그 순간 나는 회사를 그만두기로 결심했다. 내 삶에 변화가 필요하다는 걸 알았다.

- 그 순간 나는 진정으로 행복하다고 느꼈다. 아무것도 부럽지 않았다.

- 그 순간 나는 늦었다는 걸 깨달았다. 나는 최대한 빨리 뛰기 시작했다.

🫦 스피킹2_ 내 이야기해 봅시다 [해석]

질문 영어가 늘면 뭘 하고 싶으세요?

답
- 해외여행을 가서 현지인들과 영어로 대화하고 싶어요.

- 영어 원서를 읽고, 자막 없이 TED 강연을 보고 싶어요.

- 구글에서 영어로 정보를 검색하고 싶어요.

- 영어로 된 유튜브 채널을 이해하고 즐기고 싶어요.

제나쌤의 영어리스닝 길잡이

초판 1쇄 발행 2025년 12월 5일

지은이   제나(김주연)
책임편집   제나(김주연)
발행인   최병윤
디자인   류은혜

출판등록   2025년 5월 7일
발행처   길잡이북스
이메일   guideenglish0579@gmail.com
유튜브채널   길잡이영어
인쇄처   예림인쇄

ISBN   979-11-994591-1-3 (03740)

죽어라 안들리던 영어가 드디어 들리기 시작한다!

토종 한국인 영어강사 본인과 지난 15년간
수많은 영어학습자들의 영어 귀를 트여준 검증된 학습법

#이런 분들께 이 책과 온라인강의를 추천드립니다

✦ 영어공부 나름 십수년 했는데 실력이 제자리같은 분
✦ 특히 눈으로는 대충 알겠는데, 막상 귀로 들으면 안들리는 분
✦ 리스닝이지만 리딩과 스피킹 실력도 동시에 함께 늘리고 싶은 분
✦ 나의 삶과 내가 사는 한국에 대해 영어로 어떻게 표현하는지 배우고 싶은 분

#학생들의 강의평

여지껏 영어공부는 듣기만 하고 눈으로만 했던 공부였는데, 내 입으로 말하고 녹음하니 너무 재밌었습니다. 외국인 친구에게 들려줬더니 너무 잘한다고 칭찬 받았어요. - 에*더님

소리내어 읽기가 진짜 많은 도움이 되어서 요즘 미드볼 때 소리가 블럭화되어 뇌를 밟고 지나 가는 느낌으로 들려요. - 명*은 님

제나쌤 강의를 통해 습득된 영어표현이 현지에서 들리고, 배운 패턴문장을 적용하여 스피킹으 로 출력하는 제 모습에 깜짝 놀랐습니다. - Five *님

직접 읽어보니 자신감도 늘고, 반복하면 할 수록 잘 읽혀지고 속도도 느는게 신기했어요. 공 부하고 들으니 더 잘들렸구요. - 민*님